"*Holy Hardship* is a must [...]
of exceptional greatness. [...]
you. The examples so vividly described in the book will also bring clarity
to your walk. Pastor Anthony Dicks pulls it all together to bless God's
people. Listen to me: do yourself a favor and get the book!"

—**Pastor Kelvin Steele,** Senior Pastor, Kings Worship Center, Simpsonville, SC

"Pastor Dicks leads us through the process of dealing with adversity
using the story of Jesus's triumphal entry into Jerusalem through his
death and resurrection. His perspective offers an opportunity to see
adversity in a new light. His focus on patience, trust, and prayer gives
healthy Christian guidelines for living through pain and loss with clear
Christian hope at the end."

—**Pastor Mike Flanigan,** Holy Cross Episcopal Church, Simpsonville, SC

"Dr. Dicks shares the timeless truths adversity has taught him and how
these principles have transformed his life. His ability to explain the
advantages of adversity is beyond outstanding and promises to be the
difference maker in the lives of those who read this life-changing work."

—**Rev. Dr. Emory Berry Jr.,** Senior Pastor, Greenforest Community Baptist
Church, Decatur, GA

"In a culture that highlights the accouterments of success, we rarely talk
about the reality of pain, loss, stress, and hardships. In this book Pastor
Dicks will not only provide you incredible insight to overcome and
thrive amid adversity but will give you the tools to identify and classify
the adversity you are facing. May the revelations within guide and guard
you through your holy hardships!"

—**Rev. Dr. Charles E. Goodman Jr.,** Senior Pastor, Tabernacle Baptist Church,
Augusta, GA

"Despite the obstacles that have been presented to Reverend A. A. Dicks
Jr., he has managed to turn lemons into lemonade and teach us how to
do the same without becoming bitter. Reverend Dicks's testimony and
nuggets of wisdom breathe life to the reader. Page after page, the reader
is drawn in until the wounds of their life experience are healing."

—**Bishop Carl D. Parrott,** Senior Pastor of Rhema Word Restoration Ministries,
Presiding Prelate, T.R.U.E. Fellowship

"This book is excellent. It will 'scratch where most of us itch.' A few times
I had to put the book down and reflect how I handled challenges in my
ministry. Was Jesus my model or was I trying to be like someone else?"

—**Rev. Dr. William Flippin,** Senior Pastor, Greater Piney Grove Baptist Church,
Atlanta, GA

"This is a must-read for everyone who needs the right language and tools to grow beyond their adversity. It possesses the perfect balance of theological depth coupled with enlightening practicality. Dicks has embraced the role to mentor his readers into a new relationship with adversity to find the purpose beyond their pain."

—**Pastor Travis Simons,** MDiv, Associate Pastor, The Potter's House North Dallas, Frisco, TX

"The earnest offering in these pages is the sacred sentiments of a pastor who is deeply acquainted with the joys, rewards, and sorrows of every season of life. This book is theologically rich, intellectually accessible, and practically relevant. You will be captivated and comforted by these transformative teachings. The thoughts here are mined from a deep well of experience and satisfyingly saturated with love, wisdom, and grace."

—**Rev. Sheleta E. Fomby,** New Life Church, Laurel, MD

"I have known Anthony for several years and his is a true and authentic faith that has been tested. In *Holy Hardship*, he gives you a peak into how he journeyed through an excruciating season of testing and trial. All of us will go through a season of testing, and Anthony blesses us with the wisdom of one who has gone before."

—**Erik Ely,** President, Tre Fratelli Consulting, Columbia, SC

"Anthony Dicks does not disappoint. He has found a way to marry the intellectual, informative, and inspirational. *Holy Hardship* is scholarly in that it broadens your theological scope of adversity and its purpose in our lives. Yet, it is simplistic in that it is filled with foundational truths rooted in the gospel of Jesus Christ! It is definitely worth reading!"

—**Barry J. Elliot,** The Logos Connection, Charlotte, NC

"Pastor Anthony Dicks has written an amazing volume that will take you on a detailed biblical exposition that demonstrates the presence, purpose, and plan of the Divine in our human sacrifice and struggle. Be prepared: *Holy Hardship* will elevate your discipleship to the Christlike character that we all so desperately desire. It will move you to be more and more like the one who did what was hard to make us holy."

—**Rev. Dr. Carolyn Ann Knight,** Atlanta, GA

"This book is authentic, transparent, and full of wisdom that gives the reader insight and understanding into the meaningfulness of adversity. The words come to life as Dicks shares how he has personally navigated difficult times. This book will change the way you look at adversity."

—**Pastor Simeon Moultrie,** Senior Pastor, The Brook, Columbia, SC

HOLY
HARDSHIP

ANTHONY A. DICKS JR.

HOLY
HARDSHIP

HOW JESUS TURNS YOUR

ADVERSITY INTO AN ADVANTAGE

LEAFWOOD
PUBLISHERS
an imprint of Abilene Christian University Press

HOLY HARDSHIP

How Jesus Turns Your Adversity into an Advantage

L E A F W O O D
P U B L I S H E R S
an imprint of Abilene Christian University Press

Published in association with Jevon Bolden of the Embolden Media Group, PO Box 953607, Lake Mary, FL 32795.

Cataloging-in-Publication Data is on file at the Library of Congress, Washington, DC.

Cover design by Greg Jackson, ThinkPen Design, LLC
Interior text design by Sandy Armstrong, Strong Design

Leafwood Publishers is an imprint of Abilene Christian University Press
ACU Box 29138
Abilene, Texas 79699

1-877-816-4455
www.leafwoodpublishers.com

22 23 24 25 26 27 28 / 7 6 5 4 3 2 1

CONTENTS

WHY ME?

There was a man in Bethlehem who had seven sons. He really had eight. Unfortunately, the youngest son was not counted among the others for questionable reasons. On normal days, the distinction between the other seven and the last-born son was not as stark. All of that changed the day the prophet Samuel came to the house of Jesse.

There was a multitude of mixed emotions the morning that Samuel was heard to be journeying to Jesse's house. Seven of the sons of Jesse were ready to be seen by the prophet, but they did not know why. The unknown reason for the visit was the culprit for such a plethora of emotions. The seven sons were anxious, excited, expectant, and reluctant, all at the same time. The youngest boy, however, was relaxed. He was used to being discounted and rejected. He had grown accustomed to being left out of the most important events and activities of the house. His day was just like any other. At least, that was how his day started.

Can you imagine what David's emotions were like when he received the message in the sheepfold that the prophet Samuel wanted to see him? Put yourself in his shoes. David was purposely not included in the lineup of sons. As the youngest son, he did not have the favor of Joseph the son of Jacob, nor a coat of many colors. He always came last. You can imagine that David, after years of rejection and alienation, resolved that his lot in life was to always be last. If you were treated by your father like David was treated by his, you would have received the news of the prophet's desire by asking yourself, "Why me?"

David may have said those words to himself when he heard that the prophet specifically asked for him, the youngest son. David's own father did not call for him. Imagine the nervous angst David exhibited when he walked into the room that day. He may have walked into the room to see the dejection of his brothers, the bewilderment of his father, and the intense stare of the prophet. Everyone in the room was waiting on him. No one in the room knew why.

At this point, the prophet called David forward. David had to be shaking on the inside. The all too familiar "heart sinking into stomach" had happened much more frequently in the last few minutes than it had during his whole life. Samuel, after calling him forward, asked him to kneel. In the modern vernacular, "things just got real."

David knelt and closed his eyes. At that point, he would have been the only one in the room in that position. All eyes were on Samuel. Samuel's eyes were on David. Suddenly, all the air left the room. The seven older sons of Jesse were visibly distraught and surprised. Jesse must have braced himself to keep from fainting. Samuel reached under his mantle and pulled out the horn of oil he used to anoint priests and the current king.

The boys and their father knew that David was not being anointed priest, because he was not part of the tribe of Levi. They were taken aback, however, because of all the sons of Jesse, it was David who was being anointed as the next king.

David, again, was the last to know. He had his eyes closed so he could not tell what was going on. After what seemed like the longest minute in his life, he felt something on his head. It felt thick, like an ointment. No sooner than he felt the oil, he smelled the fragrance of the holy anointing oil penetrating the smell of the sheep he had grown accustomed to.

If you have ever read 1 Samuel 16, you would probably agree that this was a turning point in the family of Jesse. After seeing the prophet pour the holy anointing oil on David's head, the entire room may have asked the same question: Why him? David's question from the sheepfold had yet to be answered and was repeated: Why me?

On that day, David went from being last in his family to being the prognosticated first in the kingdom. David was designated to assume the highest office in the kingdom of Israel. The story of David lets us know that there are some blessings and opportunities that come into your life that make you ask yourself, "Why me?"

David was chosen to go from anonymity to notoriety. He was destined for greatness. He was called to be a king. Unfortunately for him, the anointing he received that day made him aware of the call to the throne but did not provide any indications as to what the call would cost him. David eventually discovered what you may be experiencing right now. In the seventeen years between David receiving the anointing to be king and sitting on the throne as king of Israel, he learned that an anointing that makes you ask "Why me?" also comes with adversity that makes you ask the same question.

Between chapter 17 of 1 Samuel and chapter 5 of 2 Samuel, David experienced a smorgasbord of adversity. He faced a giant everyone else was afraid to fight. He was vehemently pursued by Saul, the jealous sitting king of Israel. His wife and children were kidnapped, and his home was burned to the ground by the Amalekites. The adversity David faced was not because of his sin. On his way to the throne, David did not suffer as a sinner; he suffered as a servant.

This book is for people who have been called to do something phenomenal and be someone great but are suffering. You are not suffering because of sin, but because of your service. You are praying and asking God, "Why me? Why are they after me? Why am I going through this?" You cannot seem to figure out why you have all this potential and promise, and, at the same time, face a ton of problems.

Allow me to ease some of your frustration. The reason David faced adversity on the way to the throne is the same reason you are facing adversity on the way to becoming who God called you to be. David experienced hardship, and aspects of his life were to foreshadow the life of our Lord. Our Lord can kill our Goliaths, but he also knows what it is like to be persecuted because of envy, and he knows how to recover after being ambushed by his adversaries.

You are experiencing challenges because, as a disciple of Jesus, you represent Christ to the world. People should not only be able to see Jesus through your holiness, but also through your hardships. You are not in the throes of adversity because of what you have done; you are in a crucible of challenges because of who you are and who you are called to become.

You are becoming more like Jesus. Jesus already knows what it is like to be you. Your hardship as a disciple comes so that you might know what is like to be him. In fact, I would suggest that hardship is one of the ways you become like Jesus.

The Advantage of Adversity

A year I will never forget is 2017. I was pastoring a growing and vibrant church. The church had experienced the best year of its existence, according to my success metrics. I was so optimistic about 2017 for the church that I dubbed the year as the year for "Better."

By the third Sunday in January, all that optimism turned negative. I experienced the worst few months of my pastoral career during the next few weeks. The adversity intensified during Lent and would not subside until after Pentecost.

After leading the church to levels of influence it had not experienced before, I was almost voted out as pastor. There were petitions, closed-door meetings, specially called church meetings, and much more that I experienced from February to May 2017.

I had not stolen any money or failed morally. My job and ministry were being attacked because of how I served, not because I had sinned. I could not understand why I was going through what I was going through. People I served, prayed for, ministered to, empowered, and cared for took measures to assassinate my character and significantly handicap my career.

I was conspired against. My character was publicly defamed. At the church meeting held to decide my fate, there was a letter distributed that listed all the grievances and accusations against me. I was not a perfect pastor, but I was not as bad as I was being portrayed. I was in trouble—real trouble.

What I learned through those months led me to write this book. I learned that trouble changes you. The only question is, who will trouble turn you into? I also learned that, when trouble comes, it's not about how things turn out but who you turn into that matters the most. Adversity can be advantageous if you handle it right.

It may not seem this way to you, but it is true that there is an advantage in your adversity. Your adversity has an advantage in it if two things are in place. First, there is an advantage in adversity if your hardship takes the form of a cross. Second, there is an advantage in your adversity if you take the form of Christ.

Cross-shaped adversity is hardship that involves conflict with human ideas, institutions, and individuals because of a call from God. David's conflict with Saul was because of his call from God. Joseph's conflict with his brothers was because of a dream from God. Paul's conflict with the Jews in Jerusalem was because of his call from God. Jesus was not crucified because of his sin but because of envy. He was not crucified because of what he had done but because of who he claimed to be. The type of adversity I am alluding to is the kind where obedience to God is causing conflict with men. It is the kind of trouble God gets you into. He does not prevent it—rather, he permits it.

The good news is that cross-shaped adversity can transform you from a shepherd to a king, a dreamer to a prince, a crucified Nazarene into one who has all power in heaven and on earth. Within the crucible of trial that comes along with cross-shaped adversity is the opportunity to become more than you were before the adversity. The advantage of adversity does not promise that things will ever get back to the way they were before. The advantage promises that you and your circumstances will be better than normal when things do not look like they will ever get back to normal.

To experience the advantage of adversity, you not only need to experience cross-shaped trouble, but you must handle that trouble like Christ. You can move from trauma to triumph if you handle your hardship like Jesus handled his. If you can do that, you not only grow closer to Jesus's presence, but you can also grow closer to being like him as a person. Your adversity can work to your advantage if you allow it to transform you into a person like Christ.

I knew I had reaped the advantage of adversity when I was sharing with a pastoral colleague my thoughts about my situation. While riding in Atlanta with him that day, he said, "Rev., you should write a book about this, because the perspective you gained would help a lot of people."

This book seeks to give perspective on your problems and pain. There is more to your hardship than adverse circumstances. Your adversity can give you an advantage if you handle it like Jesus. To show you how to handle your adversity and grow into a more Christlike person, I am going to use the passion narratives of Jesus. Jesus not only saved us from sin on his cross; he also showed us the way to allow adversity to transform us into better people.

I do not want adversity to get the best of you. I want you to get the best of it. Your challenges and trials are offering you an advantageous opportunity to become better instead of bitter. To take advantage of your trial in such a way that it transforms you for the better, you must see Jesus as a model to follow, which is more than merely a master to obey. I hope this book encourages you to pick up your cross and follow him because you can see the advantage of adversity.

JESUS, YOUR TEACHER TO FOLLOW

Those who know me know I love to watch movies. That is one of my favorite things to do. I am an avid consumer of media. My mom would often tell me while I was growing up that I was a good baby; all she had to do was sit me in front of a television with a warm bottle, and she would not have to worry about me moving out of that spot *ever*.

Since my early childhood, the "picture box" has captivated my attention. One genre of film, gangster movies, continues to keep my attention. *Reservoir Dogs*, *The Godfather*, *Scarface*, *Hoodlum*, *The Departed*, *The Untouchables*, *Carlito's Way*, and even *Dick Tracy* are some of the best movies I have ever enjoyed. The accents, regalia, coded speech, and intensity were all intriguing to me.

One of the things I picked up about the culture of that world was the benefits and cost to being a "made man." Once you become a "made man," you become a part of the family, *La Cosa Nostra*. You receive protection and attain privilege, prestige, and responsibility. To a young disciple of a don, to hear that they were about to be a "made man" would have engendered much gratitude.

The clandestine and diabolical world of gangsters, like many twisted cultures, has a tendency to exploit and pervert the good in a person to facilitate a questionable agenda. However, I think there is something to this idea of being made. Maybe there is an innate human desire that a don, leader, or father will make something of someone.

I think that all of us, whether we are willing to admit it or not, have an innate itch that only the real Father can scratch by saying the words, "I'm going to make something out of you." There is nothing comparable to hearing the Lord say, "I will make . . ." These words instigate creation, which cause both material and immaterial objects to stand on edge. The angels gasp when they hear the creator say, "I will make . . ."

Can you imagine the excitement and astonishment when the angelic host, along with all the animals, plants, and minerals on and in the earth, heard God say in Genesis 1:26, "Let us make" and then followed it up with making humanity? According to Psalm 8:4, the angels wondered, "What is man, that though art mindful of him? and the son of man, that thou visitest him?" God took pleasure in making humanity.

It is without coincidence that after the creation of Adam, the first man, that Jesus, the last Adam, walked along a beach and said to some young fishermen, "Follow me, and I will make you" (Matt. 4:19). The Bible says that upon hearing those words, two brothers, Andrew and Simon, dropped everything and followed him. They knew nothing of Jesus's future, and they knew nothing of where this Nazarene would take them. He did not tell them where he was going. The command to follow did not come with direction, but it did promise development.

Jesus said, "Follow me, and I will make you fishers of men" (Matt. 4:19). I can imagine that Simon and Andrew were thinking to themselves, *What is a fisher of men? I've never heard of one of those before. They don't have any of those in Galilee. Never met a fisher of men before. That's a new thing.* Jesus promised to make something of the disciples that they had never seen or heard of before. They would be a new creation.

Jesus promised to lead these fishermen into a process to become fishers of men. Without presenting credentials, a curriculum vitae, a cover letter, a résumé, or a LinkedIn referral, Jesus spoke and expected a positive response. Jesus understood that these guys needed more than fish; they needed a future. There was no future in fishing for fish, but there was a future in fishing for men.

In the invitation to discipleship, Jesus told the brothers what they would do with him before he told them what he would do with them. "Follow me," which is what they were to do with him, led to "I will make you," which is what he would do with them. In other words, Jesus was saying, *If you do this with me, I will do this with you!*

Jesus's ministry with the twelve was not merely to educate them but to create something out of them. Discipleship is a process in which fellowship leads to formation. The person you follow will form you. Jesus has intentions on not only informing you but transforming you.

Bill Hull, in *The Disciple-Making Pastor*, argues that the church is called to produce disciples.[1] The church is not just an organization to make people better but to make better people. The byproduct of better people, or people made in the image of Christ, is a better world. Jesus, through his church, makes disciples. In the disciple-making process, potential disciples are tested for quality control to make sure that they are progressing through the process according to the prototype who is the Lord Jesus Christ.

Most teachers take daily attendance and give periodic tests. Most educational theorists would suggest that there is a correlation between attendance and academic performance. I am not here to argue as to whether that theory proves true. However, perfect attendance does not guarantee academic success. If it did, then there would be no tests in school; the teacher would just take attendance.

As a master teacher, Jesus understood that showing up to class was necessary but not sufficient. His disciples had to endure questioning and assessments along the journey to ensure the quality of their formation. Being with him was not enough to make them like him. Transformative discipleship requires both teaching and testing!

Jesus initiated one such test in Matthew 16. While in Caesarea Philippi, Jesus catechized the disciples with a two-question test. The questions seemed harmless enough and easy enough to answer: "Whom do men say that I the Son of man am?" (Matt. 16:13) and "Whom say ye that I am?" (Matt. 16:15). However, given the response of Jesus at the close of the exam, these questions were important to answer. Peter's answer unlocked a revelation from the teacher that marks a graduation of sorts in the narrative. Peter's answer took the formation process to another level. His answer was contingent upon who he listened to.

The first question, "Who do men say that I am?" assessed the students' listening capacity for the words of men. Who are the men you are listening to besides me? Who else has your ear? The second question assessed the disciples' capacity for balancing the words of men with the word of the Father. They knew what men said, but did they hear what God said about Jesus?

The response of Peter revealed that he heard from God. Flesh and blood did not reveal the identity of Jesus to him. Peter could not size up Jesus and conclude that he was the Son of God. Disciples learn, and they must also discern! The questions of Jesus did not just assess learning; they also assessed the disciples' openness to discerning.

Jesus responded to Peter with the revelation of the church, the keys, and, ultimately, the cross. Jesus disclosed the plans of the Father to those to whom the Spirit disclosed the identity of the Son. He disclosed this plan to the entire class, even though only one student provided the answer. Why did the others remain silent? Did they sense the same thing that Peter did? The text seems to suggest that after seeing all the miracles that Jesus worked, after hearing the greatest sermon of all time, the Sermon on the Mount, most of the people following Jesus closely did not know who he really was.

On top of that, the disciples who were called to "follow me" had been doing so without the information that Jesus revealed after Peter's confession. They were following Jesus without knowing where he was going. You may say that that takes faith, and it did. I would argue that it takes more faith to follow Jesus to a cross than it does to follow him without knowing where he is going.

Jesus did not mention his cross to the disciples until after Peter's confession. The prediction of his passion and resurrection was hidden to the twelve until then. Peter's confession unlocked the mystery of their formation process. To be formed into the likeness of Jesus meant you had to follow him and have fellowship with him and his cross. Jesus's disclosure of his destiny tested their faith after his questions tested their discernment.

Peter's response to Jesus's disclosure of the cross indicated a profound lapse in his judgment. He could discern Jesus's hidden identity, but he could not discern the Father's hidden intent. It is commendable to know who Jesus is, but it is wise to understand the intentions of his Father. Peter could not reconcile the connection between Jesus's kingdom and Jesus's cross. In Peter's mind, and no doubt in the minds of the other disciples, kings did not carry crosses.

Peter may have experienced some intellectual dissonance due to this experience. He had been promised kingdom keys simply by confession. Jesus, however, professed that he would secure a crown by crucifixion. It suffices to say that it is easier to get keys than it is to get crowns. In other words, gaining access is easier than gaining authority. The Jesus model, the Christian model, is that influence or authority always comes with a cross. As the hymn writer Thomas Shepherd once wrote, "Must Jesus bear the cross alone and all the world go free? No there's a cross for everyone and there's a cross for me."[2]

Up to this point in their formation process, the disciples had heard the call of discipleship and responded well.

They had learned the cost of a crown and stumbled through the course. They may have failed the test of discerning the wisdom of God, but their faith still had them following Jesus after learning about his cross. Isn't it good to know that even if you fail on one level, your faith can keep you in the process to reach the next level! You can keep the keys if you just keep the faith!

I would encourage you to learn from the disciples—answering the call to discipleship requires that you not only submit to Jesus's crown but also commit to his cross. Jesus tried to tell the disciples this when he predicted his suffering and death. Given Peter's response to that revelation, Jesus waited to tell them what the kingdom would cost the disciples. They knew what the kingdom would cost Jesus, but they still did not know what it would cost them. They had heard preaching about the kingdom, but not the price! As a senior leader in a church, I have become all too aware of the difference between the preaching of the kingdom and the price of the kingdom. Let me just say this: given the narrative of Jesus Christ, the kingdom must be preached, and the price must be paid!

Jesus, after sharing the news of his cross with the disciples, rebuked Peter for rebuking him and disclosed the destiny of those who followed him. Jesus said to the disciples, "If any man will come after me, let him deny himself, and take up his cross, and follow me" (Matt. 16:24).

It is obvious that the teaching style and the educational philosophy of Jesus were different from the teaching approach of most modern educators. Jesus waited until the middle of the course to disclose the price of the lessons. The call of discipleship is to be with him, but the cost of discipleship is to be like him. The syllabus of discipleship has been written into a cross. Remember that discipleship, if it is Christian, is not about education, but transformation. Jesus's model suggests that transformation can only occur through fellowship. Fellowship is not only about shared philosophy, but shared experience. The chief end of discipleship is not just to be with him but to be like him in both authority and adversity.

I think that we have done the gospel a disservice if the point of our gospel is to go to heaven just to be with Jesus. The narratives of Acts and the epistles of the apostles suggest that none of them were in a rush to be with Jesus after his ascension. They were in no hurry to be in heaven with him, but they were long-suffering because they just wanted to be like him! They wanted full fellowship!

The apostle Paul put it this way in Philippians 3:10: "That I may know him, and the power of his resurrection, and the fellowship of his sufferings, being made conformable unto his death." It is of note that these words were written by someone who was not one of the twelve apostles.

Paul came into the faith years after the ascension of Jesus Christ and was only a young man at the time of the seven servants in Acts 6. It is obvious from his own words that the apostle's doctrine was not first and foremost about going to heaven to be with Jesus but about enduring the process to be like Jesus. This process included the power of the resurrection, but not without a conformable fellowship of his sufferings. The apostles were so enamored by the Christ that they wanted to be like him regardless of the cost. For them, they could not be with him if they were not like him! They could not enjoy the privilege of being with him if they did not experience the privilege of suffering like him.

This intense fidelity to the Christ was not just reserved for apostles, prophets, evangelists, pastors, teachers, elders, ministers, deacons, and other liturgical and ecclesiastical offices and posts. This intense desire for fellowship in the success and sufferings of Jesus was for all who followed him as disciples. Disciples who were called to be fishers of men were to have fellowship with him!

The narratives of Acts, along with those of the epistles, allude to an aspect of Christian discipleship that we do not embrace enough today. These texts speak of glorying in tribulation and rejoicing because one suffers for the name of Christ. The church in the apostolic age believed that there was an advantage in adversity.

Following Jesus means more than following his instructions, obeying his teachings, and overcoming temptation. It means walking in his footsteps, experiencing his cross, and operating in the power of his resurrection. The call to discipleship was not "obey me"; it was "follow me." Follow him to a garden, a trial, a cross, and a grave. It is not until you have followed him there that you can experience the transformative advantage of adversity. It is through the fellowship of suffering that you are rewarded with the advantage of adversity.

Philippians says that it was because of Jesus's obedience through the adversity of the cross that he received a name that is above any other name. Your adversity is working in your favor to make your name great. You must follow Jesus on that path and follow his pattern.

If you follow him through your hardship, you can learn how to be like him. If you follow him, it will do more for you than change your name; it will change your nature. If you follow him, you will draw closer to him in likeness, not just location. If you follow him, you will be more than convicted; you will be converted into the image of the Son of God. It will not be easy, but it will be worth it. Pick up your cross, and follow him.

NOTES

[1] Bill Hull, *The Disciple-Making Pastor* (Grand Rapids: Baker Books, 2007).

[2] Thomas Shepherd, "Must Jesus Bear the Cross Alone?" 1693.

YOUR DISCIPLESHIP—THE BIG PICTURE

Simon Peter is my favorite disciple. I cannot pinpoint one attribute that he possessed that makes him my favorite. He is not my favorite because of one act or a few sayings. He is my favorite because, like me, he struggled to be more like Jesus. One minute he was being affirmed for how he heard from the Father; the next minute he was being rebuked for being used by Satan. One minute he was walking on water, and the next minute he was sinking. Peter's story resonates with me the most because it is clear that following and being like Jesus is not easy. His story gives me hope because it is not a perfect story.

Peter had his good days and his bad days as a disciple of Jesus Christ. I am sure you agree that the same can be said for your discipleship journey. The story of Simon Peter opens our eyes to some of the intricacies and struggles of discipleship. His story gives us a snapshot of the big picture of our discipleship.

What's in a Name?

According to Matthew's Gospel, it was Peter who confessed that Jesus was the Christ, the son of the true and living God. But technically, it was Simon, according to Matthew 16:16. The confession of this revelation led to Simon's name change to Peter. Simon got a new name; he did not quite yet have a great name.

The name change episode in Matthew's Gospel leads us to ask an interesting question: To whom did Jesus promise the keys of the kingdom, Simon or Peter? The delineation and distinction that this question asks us to make unveils an opportunity to investigate further what the text may be saying between the lines. Literarily, the two names in the narrative, though they refer to the same person, identify two different characters. The two names as they are proclaimed speak to a conversion process inherent in Jesus's declaration.

If Jesus changed Simon's name to Peter, what happened to Simon? There can be no acquisition of the new without the passing away of the old. If Jesus called Peter into being, Simon had to pass away. Jesus then must have given the keys to the character of Peter. The character of Simon could not possess or use the keys.

It is possible to be promised keys that you cannot use at the time of the promise. At the time of this writing, I have two children who are of driving age. However, neither of them currently has a license. It is within my power to give them the keys to my car, but they would not be able to use the car to its maximum capacity. They would be in possession of keys that they could not employ. I could proclaim loudly and proudly that they have the keys to Daddy's car. However, without being processed and tested, they will not be able to use those keys.

It's an elementary example, but I hope you get the point. Peter may have received a promise of kingdom keys, but without being processed and tested, he could not use them. Peter could not practice what Jesus proclaimed without being processed! Please do not let the speed of the narrative and proclamation confuse you. The pericope identifies a change in name that happened in the moment. The entire narrative biography of Peter, however, suggests that it was much easier to change his name than it was to change his character. You can change a name by proclamation, but you change a character with process!

One of the challenges in modern Christian discipleship is that we often think that we can go from promise to power without process. Making a confession for Christ does not fully convert your character. Discipleship is the process by which confessed Christians are converted into people conformed into the image of Jesus Christ. Unfortunately, many people in church these days place more emphasis on confessions than conversion. Operating in the power you have been promised requires more than you naming it and claiming it. You must be converted.

Simon could not become Peter without a conversion experience. Simon's character could not handle the keys. Only someone with the characteristics of Peter could handle the responsibility and authority of the keys of the kingdom. If you were to look at the meaning of these names, you would find a clue to the progression of the future of Peter's fellowship with Jesus.

The name Jesus declared after the disciple's confession was Simon, son of Jonah. Simon is the Greek derivative of the Hebrew name Simeon, which means *he has heard*. The name Jonah comes from a Hebrew name that means *dove*. Peter is a name that means *rock*. It seems to follow then that the character who had heard from the dove (the Spirit of God) was now being formed into a rock. A rock, according to Matthew, is a foundation worthy of being built upon. Simon lived up to his former name and was now ready to be formed to live into his new name.

How are Peters formed? How are rocks formed? Each rock in the earth has distinct features and characteristics. One rock is unique to all other rocks. The uniqueness of their identifiable characteristics, shapes, textures, and sizes can be attributed to the outcome of the things the rock has been through. Rocks are formed by friction. Rocks are beaten by the dirt, sand, water, other minerals, and the other rocks that rub against it. Just as natural rocks are formed by adversity, Peter the spiritual rock would be formed by hardship.

By the time we witness the apostle Peter standing among the apostles to preach the sermon on Pentecost, he had endured his fair share of hardship and adversity. Some adversity he experienced before his name was changed, and there was some that he experienced after. Luke, however, grants us access to one adverse experience that may have actually converted Simon into Peter. I have personally experienced my fair share of adversity, and I have learned that some types of adversity only affect you, while other types of adversity change you.

When Thou Art Converted

Luke 22:31–34 is the brief episode of Jesus disclosing to Peter a piece of his future. Jesus said, "Simon, Simon, behold, Satan hath desired to have you, that he may sift you as wheat: But I have prayed for thee, that thy faith fail not: and when thou art converted, strengthen thy brethren" (Luke 22:31–32).

There is so much that could be said about this disclosure of trial. Notice the name by which Jesus spoke to his disciple. Jesus called him Simon, indicating the character that was going to undergo the "sifting." Satan was after Simon, to sift him like wheat. Sifting occurs when wheat is reaped, not sowed. In other words, sifting occurs during harvest time. Satan waits until harvest time to sift the gifted.

Sifting is a process practiced for quality control. Sifting separates the wheat from the chaff. When the sifter sifts the wheat, he throws it up in the air and allows the wind to blow the chaff away from the wheat. After the sifting process, all the chaff is gone, and all that remains is the wheat. God allowed Satan to develop the character of Simon, sifting those things that cannot be used, only to leave behind the wheat of Peter. God allowing Satan to process you for quality control will sift your faith! You know when you are in the sifting process when you say to yourself, "I can't believe God is allowing this to happen."

Can you handle a God who allows the devil to develop your character? Can you handle a Father who allows an enemy to mishandle you? Can you handle a Christ who intercedes so that you would make it through the sifting but who won't intervene to stop the sifting? Can you handle a Jesus who prays for you to endure the trial, not to avoid the trial? Can you handle a God who tells the devil yes?

In your future, you have an appointment with the sifter. The sifting will shake and shape your faith. God does not convert you conventionally. The character he wishes to develop in us requires a severe shaking that shakes us like wheat, to our very core. The good news is that we will make it through the sifting because Jesus prayed that our faith would not fail.

The sifting of Simon Peter would leave him with a faith that was stronger than his failures. He would go on to commit the faithless act of denying Jesus yet remaining faithful enough to stay in the community of disciples until the resurrection. The sifting will separate our faithless acts from our faithful attitude. The sifting converts our Simon to Peter.

Luke also gives us insight into the other components that will be tried during the process of being conformed to the image of Christ. Luke 22:62 gives us the emotional state of Peter during the sifting. The verse shares with us that after Peter denied Jesus that he "went out, and wept bitterly." This indicates that the sifting, the test, the trial, does not just try that which is spiritual. It tries more than your faith; it tries your feelings.

I will never forget a conversation I had with a dear friend of mine while I was experiencing adversity in my pastorate. I called him to vent my frustration with the situation. I was looking for comfort, solace, and sympathy. Needless to say, I did not get what I expected. My friend allowed me space to get all that I wanted to say off my chest. He then said these words: "For all these years you preached about a cross, now God has put you in a place so that you can feel what it is like to actually be on one. I wish I had other words to say to you, but all I can say to you is for this hardship, you have to feel it."

Luke indicates that the sifting is not a simulation. Sifting is not virtual; it is tangible, meaning you can feel it! The fellowship of his suffering affects you from center to circumference. The forming process will touch your body, your soul, and your spirit. The cross not only does something for your soul; it does something to your soul! Peter wept bitterly. Peter got to a place where he could deny himself only because he heard himself deny Jesus. He watched himself do things he said he would never do. In fact, according to Luke 22:61, Jesus saw Peter do what he said he would never do.

There will be times during your conversion experience when you will disappoint yourself and feel like you have disappointed Jesus. There will be times when you weep bitterly. The bitter weep of a disciple is indicative of a shifting during the sifting. Your tears are evacuating what can make you bitter so that God can make you better.

Peter's development through the Gospels and his actions during the passion of Jesus Christ indicate for us what it looks like to join the "fellowship of his sufferings" (Phil. 3:10). Peter learned that the cross you carry as a disciple is not for the devil. God is not going to crucify our enemies. As the hymn says, "there's a cross for everyone and there's a cross for me."[1] The cross was not for Satan; it was for Simon.

Peter also learned that the process of developing Christlike character cannot be read about or observed; it must be endured. You cannot simulate sifting. You have to experience it for yourself. The process must engage your emotions, your intellect, and your will. It must do something to your soul. It must engage you during harvest time, to develop a strong core when you are up and when you are down. The same devil that took Jesus to a high place takes maturing disciples to a low place. The sifting tests you at different altitudes to see if your character is influenced by the Spirit or by the fickle vacillations of your emotions.

Peter also learned another powerful lesson. He learned the power of a big-picture perspective! I believe that is one of the things that helped him endure the process of sifting and conversion. The words of Jesus Christ in Luke 22:32 provide the big-picture perspective of this prophetic conversation. Jesus said, "But I have prayed for thee, that thy faith fail not: and when thou art converted, strengthen thy brethren."

The latter clause of this saying of Jesus reveals the perspective of Jesus. Jesus says when you are converted. He does not say "if"; he says "when." This is an indication that whatever he prayed for Peter was affirmed by the Father. Jesus prayed that Peter's faith would not fail, and the word *when* indicates that it would not fail. There may have been moments during the sifting when Peter thought that he was not going to make it, but from Jesus's perspective, he was going to make it even before the process began. Jesus knew that he would go through, but he also knew that he would make it through.

The word *when* also indicates that there is an "after" to this test. The timely word *when* indicates that the sifting is temporary. The addition of the phrase "you are converted" indicates that the trouble will expire before you do, and that you will never be the same after this is over. The old you will be dead!

The pinnacle of a big-picture perspective is in the last words of Christ's statement, "strengthen thy brethren." These words bring tears to my eyes. They indicate the chief characteristic of advantageous adversity. With these words, Jesus let Peter know that what he was about to endure, that what was about to happen to him, was not for him. One endures sovereign suffering to strengthen others. The sufferings of Christ were not for him; they were for us and our salvation. Suffering that forms Christ in you is suffering that is for the sake of others; that is the big picture.

The evangelist shares with us the story of Jesus's passion so that we might gain strength and be converted. The evangelist also shares the story of Peter's struggle so we might receive strength when we are being converted. You are going to make it through this tough season because of what the evangelist has shared. You must remember the big picture. Your struggle and development is not for you. You are going through it so that after it is over, you, too, can strengthen others. You are sharing in his struggle so that when others hear you share your struggle, they can gain strength. Remember the big picture.

NOTE

[1] Thomas Shepherd, "Must Jesus Bear the Cross Alone?" 1693.

YOUR TROUBLE,
IT'S COMING

Luke opened his Gospel account with an intriguing statement. His desire was "to write an orderly account" (Luke 1:3 NIV). Does this mean that the other Gospels written at the time of Luke's writing were not orderly? Is that statement a critique of the other Gospels? Was Luke, to use a colloquial phrase, "throwing shade"?

You may look at his wording in that way, but I invite you to think about it differently. The Gospel according to Luke, it has been suggested, was written to a Greek audience. The uniqueness of this Gospel involved an attempt to herald a Jewish Messiah to a Greek audience. Luke's task was to overcome the cultural differences of those two demographics in an effort to tell Gentiles about Jesus of Nazareth.

Seeing as this Gospel is the prequel to the book of Acts, in which many read others speaking in their native tongue, maybe Luke, filled with the Holy Ghost, was sharing the gospel with Greeks in a language they could understand. Greeks understood order. Their logic, categories, philosophies, and cultural views about beauty could be said to be concerned heavily with order.

Luke seemed to be graced with the ability to speak the gospel about a Jew in a way that would intrigue any Greek. He was charged with a huge task of writing to a Greek audience about Jewish culture, ideas, and practices. This task intensified in Luke 4, where he introduced into the narrative a new character he called the devil.

Unlike many of the novels of our day, Luke did not go into much character development before this new character was introduced in the narrative. The character called "the devil" develops over the course of the narrative. By the time we get to Luke 22, "the devil" of chapter 4 has a proper name: "Satan."

Who was "the devil" or "Satan" to the Jews? What were his characteristics and common practices? An investigation into the history of this diabolical character introduced in the narrative may prove insightful regarding the timing of our adversity. Let's consider two biblical narratives about this devious character: one from Genesis and the other from Job.

My reason for choosing these two narratives is because of their age. Job is believed to be the oldest book in the Bible, and it offers some insight into what ancient people, especially the Jews, thought of Satan. Genesis, though considered younger than Job, is about an older story than Job. Genesis's account of the serpent (a type of Satan) is about the first encounter men had with the devil, thereby offering keen insight into the character and practices of Satan. As my mama would say, "The devil ain't got no new tricks." If we can examine the enemy in his narrative infancy, we will gain much help in overcoming his wiles.

A broad approach to examining the narratives of Genesis 3 and Job 1 yields an interesting discovery. The settings of these narratives are different, but the character Satan, or the serpent, is the same. In Genesis 3, we see the serpent in the Garden with man. In Job 1, we see him in the king's court in heaven with God. In Genesis 3, the serpent talked to men about God. In Job 1 and 2, he talked to God about men. These differences are helpful, but they do not advance our inquiry. What is more telling about Satan in these two texts is how Satan's behavior was similar.

In both these narratives, which account for some of the oldest stories about Satan, he was an antagonist and adversary between God and humanity. Job's account says that Satan, before this meeting in heaven, was "going to and fro in the earth, and from walking up and down in it" (Job 1:7). What was he doing all that walking for? Genesis helps us answer that question. In Genesis 3, the devilish character was in the Garden. The serpent was thought to have legs, and he was walking around with purpose before he encountered Eve.

Satan went "to and fro in the earth," "walking up and down in it" (Job 1:7) looking for something and someone. I would suggest that he was looking for someone to try, and the one thing he looked for in order to try someone was opportunity. Satan is searching for an opportunity to try humanity. The identifying characteristic of the devil, Satan, is that he is an opportunist.

He is always looking for a way into our lives. Any temptation is an examination for an invitation into our lives. If he has been going to and fro and walking up and down the earth, it suggests that he has not found a resting place. He is relentless in his search for anyone who will give him place to rest. If resisted, he will flee, but we must be careful, as told in the words of the apostolic warning, "Neither give place to the devil" (Eph. 4:27). We must understand that if we give him a place to rest, we will not be able to!

The opportunistic character of the devil gives us a better understanding of the temptation of Christ. The incarnation gave the devil an opportunity to tempt an intriguing new human, one the world had never seen before, the Son of God. In the heavens, he could not find a place to tempt God, but now that the Son of God had assumed flesh on earth, he had an opportunity to secure a resting place.

The devil in Genesis 3 subtly deceived humanity out of its dominion over the earth. The canon is clear that dominion over earth would not satisfy the devil; he also wanted dominion over heaven. If he could find a place in Jesus, the Son of God, maybe the old trick in the Garden would work in the wilderness, and Jesus would forfeit his dominion to him. The temptation of Jesus was the devil's attempt to take Jesus's place. The devil is an opportunist and a supplanter. He is looking for opportunities to take our place of peace, authority, power, dominion, influence, and gifting. The devil does not want you to be who God made you to be because he would rather be who God made you to be. We must be quite valuable and powerful, because the devil wants to be like us!

It is clear from Luke 4 that none of the devil's tricks worked on Jesus. At every point the devil tried to find a place in Jesus, he was soundly resisted. Jesus resisted him, and the devil fled. The resistance of Jesus proved that the devil could be overcome and resisted. Where Adam failed, Jesus prevailed. Jesus himself said that he passed the devil's examination by temptation. During the Last Supper, Jesus exclaimed that "the prince of this world cometh, and hath nothing in me" (John 14:30).

The episode in the wilderness ends with these words in Luke 4:13: "When the devil had finished every test, he departed from him until an opportune time" (Luke 4:13 NRSV). How is this possible? How could he be finished with every test and there still be an "opportune time"? The Spirit of God gave him opportunity to test. The Son of God passed the test, seemingly leaving no opportunity to the devil. If the Son wouldn't give him another opportunity, and if the Spirit wouldn't give him another opportunity, how could the devil find "an opportune time"?

At this point, we may want to revisit our earlier tandem texts of Genesis 3 and Job 1 and 2. This time, we must examine these texts not for what they tell us about Satan, but for what they help us discover about God.

Accept what God Allows

When we examine these two narratives together, we find that Satan has limited authority. The story of Job suggests, as does the story of Peter for that matter, that Satan must ask permission or be given permission to try a person. This seems to suggest that Satan petitions God for opportunities to try, tempt, and test people.

What concerns me or, at minimum, makes me uncomfortable, is that God, according to Job, Jesus, and Genesis, grants opportunity to Satan to try, test, and tempt his children. How else do we explain the presence of a snake in the Garden? God allowed the devil into paradise! The God of Genesis and Job allowed the antagonistic asp to afflict the men and women he created. Adam and Job did not give Satan an opportunity; God did!

In Job's case, we hear the conversation between God and Satan, only to find that in this case, Satan did not ask for Job; rather, God volunteered Job. He offered Job up to be tried. Job had done nothing wrong. Job had done nothing diabolical to deserve being afflicted by the devil. He was an upright, righteous man who was prosperous and affluent. He ruled his own house well and kept his children in subjection with all gravity.

The context of Job, according to many biblical scholars, is a polemic contrast to the book of Proverbs. The book of Proverbs is a work of wisdom that advocates the theology of two ways. Proverbs uses the Hebrew poetic style of parallelism to offer to the reader or hearer a stark contrast between the way of the righteous and the way of the unrighteous.

Reading the poetic book of Proverbs in isolation may lead one to think that living righteously will prevent suffering. This possible conclusion receives a sober "not so fast" from the writer of Job. The book of Job shows us that the righteous suffer, and not arbitrarily. The righteous suffer because they are righteous.

The author of Job was a great storyteller. Readers of Job, like viewers of a movie in a theater, are privileged with information that many of the main characters in the narrative do not know. The conversation in heaven between Satan and God is shared with the reader. Job had no clue that he was being volunteered by God to be tested by Satan. Job would have experienced the sudden tribulation as a surprise. It would have felt to him like all this calamity was coming out of nowhere.

When asked, "Hast thou considered my servant Job?" (Job 1:8), Satan replied that when he went to Job, he found something protecting Job. Satan answers God by questioning him, asking, "Hast not thou made an hedge about him, and about his house, and about all that he hath on every side?" (Job 1:10). Job may not have known that God had a hedge of protection around him. One definition of the term *hedge* is restraint. When Satan visited Job, his house, and all that he had, he was greeted by a hedge of restraint, a hedge of resistance. He could find no way in. Because of the hedge, the devil could find no place.

Anyone reading Job could interpret the failure of Satan to find a place of entry and access to Job as a direct result of the success of the work of God, not the work of Job. Job did not make the hedge; God did. Job was not protected by his works, but by God. Job did not work for the hedge; the hedge worked for him. Job's righteousness did not make the hedge; the Bible says that God made the hedge, a hedge so impenetrable that not even the devil, with all his devices and cunningness, could find a way in.

You and I having this privileged information about the origin and presence of the hedge, unlike Job, would be humbled upon the discovery that God made the hedge. We would no longer trust in our righteousness to protect us. I want you to understand this clearly—living righteously and living a holy life does not make a hedge of protection. God makes the hedge. You cannot live holily enough to cover all your house and everything that you have. You cannot build a righteous résumé compelling enough to warrant a hedge of protection to be given to you. The hedge is a gift of grace.

Our righteous living honors the hedge God has made; it does not create the hedge. You cannot build the hedge with righteousness; you can, however, destroy it with unrighteousness. This reality adds more intensity to the narrative because Job was not guilty of unrighteousness. God built the hedge, and because of Job's righteousness and exemplary character, he was volunteered by God to be tried by Satan. God had to move the hedge for Satan to try Job. The Lord giveth the hedge, and the Lord taketh away.

All the other times Satan tried to get to Job and could not, but this time, he found a way in—a way that God, not Job, had made. This time, Satan had an opportunity. God created an opportune time for Satan to return into Job's life. This time, Satan would not be resisted by the hedge; this time, Satan's wiles would be irresistible in a sense. Job could not stop it, and God would not stop it. God had granted Satan an opportune time, a time that would not feel that opportune to Job, a time that would come as a surprise to Job, as a threat, as disappointment, filled with pain and grief. God knew what time it was for Job. Satan knew what time it was for Job. These facts did not help Job because Job had no clue that God saw fit for the devil to try him and test him in this way. Job may have thought, *After all I have done right, why is all this stuff going wrong? Why do bad things happen to good people?*

It is not within the scope of this book to answer those questions, so I will not offer any. However, as I attempt to give perspective, I think it is helpful for you to understand that your introduction into the fellowship of his suffering will come because of God trusting you not with success but with suffering. I am not saying that God will not make you successful, wealthy, or prosperous. I am saying that you cannot determine your rightness with God or your closeness to God by the presence of success or the absence of suffering. I would like to offer the perspective that maybe God trusted Job with that level of success because he could trust Job with that level of suffering! God trusted that Job would be tried, and yet he would still trust God!

As you grow and mature as a Christian, you will find that things go awry at the most inopportune times. May I suggest that what you are perceiving as inopportune to you on earth may be an opportune time for God in heaven. For the things you face, have faced, and will face in the future, remember that God must trust you with that kind of adversity. He trusts that no matter how cursed you feel, you will not curse him. He trusts that no matter how bad it gets, you will still bless the Lord at all times. God trusts your trust in him! You have gotten through all the other trials by your faith in God, so I am asking you to consider that you may have to make it through this season of sovereign suffering because of God's faith in you!

It's Your Season
Luke 4:13 uses the word *opportune* to describe the time. The Greek word used for *opportune* is *kairos*. Paul Tillich offers a wonderful exposition on the meaning of the word *kairos* in his book, *A History of Christian Thought*:

Paul speaks of *kairos* in describing the feeling that the time was ripe, mature, or prepared. This Greek word is an example of the richness of the Greek language in comparison with the poverty of modern languages. We have only one word for "time." The Greeks had two words, *chronos* and *kairos*. *Chronos* is clock time, time which is measured, as we have it in words like "chronology" and "chronometer." *Kairos* is not a quantitative time of the clock but the qualitative time of the occasion, the right time (Cf. Its use in some of the Gospel stories.) There are things that happen when the right time, the *kairos*, has not yet come. *Kairos* makes an action possible or impossible. We all experience moments in our lives when we feel that now is the right time to do something, now we are mature enough, now we can make the decision. This is the *kairos*. It was in this sense that Paul and the early church spoke of the *kairos*, the right time for the coming of Christ."[1]

What you are experiencing or the things you may have experienced may not have felt right, but thanks be unto God it happened at the right time. The answer to your "why now?" questions is, *It's the right time*. The opportune time is another way of saying, *It's your season*.

In my tenure as a preacher and pastor, I have been afforded the wonderful opportunity to hear some of the best preachers and sermons ever. At The Meeting Place Church of Greater Columbia, South Carolina, Rev. Matthew L. Watley once shared a sermon from Luke 22 and Genesis 22 that compared the events of Abraham and Isaac on the mountain with the experience of Jesus in the Garden. In both texts, he shared that there was an interesting interaction between fathers and sons. Both the interactions were intense; however, they had two different outcomes. I was fascinated by this sermon because, at that time, I had not heard the two texts preached in juxtaposition, which is a phenomenal hermeneutical and homiletical tactic and strategy. I spent much of the sermon trying to figure out how Rev. Watley would resolve the tension of a father about to sacrifice his son in Genesis 22 and in Luke 22, because, after all, there was no ram in the bush for Jesus.

Rev. Watley "pressed his claim" (a phrase used basically to mean he argued his premise with great intensity) and drew to a close. As he pressed his claim, he shared with us the resolve. Isaac and Jesus were partakers of grace, but of two different varieties. Isaac partook of grace to escape. Jesus partook of grace to endure. Isaac's grace would get him out, but Jesus's grace would get him through.

I was floored; I had never heard grace nuanced like that. That one sentence has ministered to me for the last decade or more, especially in seasons when heaven knew but I did not know that it was an opportune time. During the opportune time, it is important to remember that the sufficiency of grace is not limited to getting us out of trouble.

Most of us love a grace that has power to rescue us. However, biblical grace, especially grace that is revealed as sufficient, is not a rescuing grace but an enduring grace. We discover that God's "grace is sufficient" in 2 Corinthians 12:9, when Paul entreated the Lord, in many ways like Jesus did in the Garden, not for the removal of a cup but the removal of the thorn. Paul received a similar response from God that Jesus did that faithful Thursday night two thousand years ago. God told the agonizing apostle that he would not remove the thorn but that he would give Paul the grace to endure it. If you are in a season when God is inducting you into this beloved fellowship of suffering to experience the advantage of adversity, take heart, because he would not do it without giving you an enduring grace.

This nuance about grace does not betray or contradict the Augustinian definition of the term as unmerited favor. Enduring grace expands the borders of the experience of grace beyond the normal and conventional approach many of us take to grace. Many of us, especially me, think of grace as unmerited favor to escape trouble or secure success. I still hold to this ideology. Grace does secure success that you do not deserve and rescues us from situations and circumstances that we do not deserve to escape. Enduring grace suggests that grace is for more than rescue and success you do not deserve.

In the same way we are graced for success we do not deserve, grace can cause you to be favored to suffer things you do not deserve. During the opportune time, you will suffer things you do not deserve. During the opportune time, you will resist the devil, and he will not flee! You must rest assured that, no matter how dark it gets, you will say, in the end, "'Tis grace that brought me safe thus far and grace will lead me home."[2]

NOTES

[1] Paul Tillich, *A History of Christian Thought: From Its Judaic and Hellenistic Origins to Existentialism* (New York: Simon & Schuster, 1972).

[2] John Newton, "Amazing Grace," 1779.

YOUR CELEBRATION, INTERRUPTED

The devil is an opportunist. In our last reading of Luke, we saw that he left our Lord until an opportune time. This same antagonist in Luke 22 is no longer called "the devil" but is called Satan. The progression of the adversary's character reminds me of the progression of Sauron in J. R. R. Tolkien's book and movie series *The Hobbit*.

In *The Hobbit*, the evil darkness that looms throughout the trilogy is first exposed as the necromancer—disguised, concealed, and deceptive. One of the characters in the movie says that he is not what he says he is. The necromancer fancied himself to be thought of as a human but concealed his true intentions until his plans of destruction and death were more mature and complete.

Eventually, through warfare and confrontation with the light of Gandalf, the necromancer was revealed to be the evil king Sauron. Sauron, once thought to be defeated, had come back to Middle-earth at a more opportune time. This fictional progression is akin to the progression of the spiritual antagonist of Luke's narrative. Within eighteen chapters, the one who started as "the devil" has grown to be revealed as Satan himself.

Luke 22:3 starts with a pregnant phrase, "Then entered Satan." We can be tempted to focus solely on what follows that phrase and deal with the one whom Satan entered. Instead of dealing with the who of Judas, let's explore the timing of the phrase "Then entered Satan."

The "then" of the text implies a unique timing to the tactic of the adversary. In the last chapter, we learned that there is an opportune time, but what does the opportune time look like? The first verse of chapter 22 is pregnant with perspective to give us a clue into the profile of the opportune time. It says, "Now the feast of unleavened bread drew nigh, which is called the Passover" (Luke 22:1).

Opportune Celebrations

Luke 22:1–3 marks a decided shift in the Lukan narrative of the Lord Jesus Christ. Unlike other synoptic Gospels, Luke's approach includes only one trip to the holy city of Jerusalem during the festival of Passover. His intent for doing this was to create literary climax. The narrative structure of Luke suggests that the opportune time at which the enemy returned was also a time of celebration in Israel.

Jerusalem is the highest point in Israel. Anyone attempting to travel there by foot would be traveling uphill to the summit of the nation. This city provides the setting of the sufferings of Jesus Christ. Geographically, Jesus was not in a valley during his passion but at the highest point in the nation. It may be the same with you during your induction into the fellowship. The opportune time may be when you finally get on top of things.

Luke 22:1 points out something else significant about the timing of the passion of Jesus Christ. It occurred during the Festival of Unleavened Bread. The Festival of Unleavened Bread, also called the Passover, was actually two commemorative celebrations culturally combined in one. Traditionally, the Festival of Unleavened Bread preceded Passover and was celebrated separately. However, the cultural setting of Jesus's day had led people to celebrate both festivals together.

The Passover was the most significant feast on the calendar of Israel. It was the commemoration of that faithful night in Egypt that sealed the deliverance of Israel from the afflicting slavery of Pharaoh. The historical event of Passover was integral in shaping the culture and identity of the nation of Israel. It was so important that God himself gave instruction on when to celebrate it and how to celebrate it. Passover was a big deal to Israel.

The importance of the Passover indicates that the timing of Jesus's passion was also culturally significant. Jesus would begin his suffering in a high place during a high time. His passion would be significant, and it would not be secret.

The festival would draw Jews from all over the world. The city would be overflowing with people. There would be a buzz in the city because of the nature of the festival that involved the expectation for a deliverer. The festival awakened in the present a hope for the future because of what God had done in the past. There would be some in the crowd that gathered in Jerusalem who hoped for the promised deliverer. There would be others actively trying to play that role, seeking opportunity to overthrow Rome.

Due to the fickle peace in Jerusalem during this festival, there would be a tremendous presence of the enforcers of the Pax Romana, the Roman soldiers. Rome had a vested interest in maintaining order in the city, especially during this feast. They were at the ready to quash any hint of rebellion.

They also wanted to provide peace due to the amount of commerce the city would experience during this feast. The amount of people coming to the city promised to bring prosperity to the region and to the empire. One entity would be grossly affected because of the festival, more than any other institution, and that was the temple. The Passover was a national festival, but it was also a religious celebration. The Jews came to celebrate their God, and they believed that their God lived in the temple in Jerusalem.

The temple guards and authorities and the chief priest and religious elite would be at the pinnacle of their influence during this festival. They would have the most influence on the people and the most influence with Roman officials during this time. Their focus was not keeping the people holy during this consecrated time, but keeping the people happy. The Romans and the religious elite knew all too well that there is a thin line between the cheers of the crowd and the madness of the mob.

It was in this context that Jesus entered Jerusalem, to the cheers of the crowd. Jesus entered the highest place of Israel, during the highest time of year, with all eyes on Jerusalem, including the religious elites and the Roman Empire, to the sound of celebration. Heralded by the crowd, "Blessed be the King that cometh in the name of the Lord" (Luke 19:38), Jesus made his entry into Jerusalem from the Mount of Olives to a congregation of celebrants. It was indeed celebration time!

Jesus, however, understood that the celebrants, the conspirators, the crowds, and the overarching cultural significance of this Passover would converge into a controversy and conflict. Jesus knew that celebration time was also the opportune time.

Sober Celebrations

One of the great contradictions of the fellowship of Jesus's suffering is that the passion ensued when Jesus had something to legitimately celebrate. Your induction into the fellowship could come during a time of celebration. My induction began when the organization I led was at the height of its influence and visibility. We had raised more money than we ever had. We had completed a building project that moved us into the twenty-first century, and we had done it debt-free. Our social media footprint was one of the largest in our region, and we had no indication of slowing down.

I had legitimate reasons to celebrate. You may have legitimate reasons to celebrate. Maybe you are at the top of your class academically. Maybe you are at the height of your approval ratings politically. Some of you may be celebrating the birth of children or your first year of marriage. My advice to you is celebrate! Participate in the celebration, but not as others do.

Many of the people in Jerusalem for Passover would celebrate with strong drink. During the wedding at Cana and the Feast of Pentecost, wine was present and prevalent. I can imagine that during the Passover there would be some who enjoyed some indulgences with wine. Others may have become intoxicated. You, like Jesus, must celebrate differently. You should celebrate your successes and the successes of others. My counsel is, regardless of what you celebrate, do so soberly.

You must stay sober because there are so many people around you who are drunk. I use the word *drunk* here as a metaphor, not to be taken literally. You can be intoxicated by things that are not liquid. As a matter of fact, one of the words for alcoholic beverages is *spirits*. People can be intoxicated with many things, and most secure their drug of choice during very low lows and very high highs!

Be aware of your surroundings during times of celebration. There are some who become intoxicated with fame and celebrity during times of celebration. There are others who become intoxicated with influence. Others become intoxicated with jealousy and envy. There are still yet others who become intoxicated with shock. Fear, lust, insecurity, jealousy, and immaturity are powerful intoxicants.

You must understand that there are some people who cannot celebrate soberly. Your responsibilities, role, influence, and authority as a son or daughter of God require that you stay sober.

Paul told Timothy that an elder in the Lord's church must not be given to wine, and then he told Timothy that a potential elder must be sober. I do not think Paul was repeating himself. Paul knew that sobriety of mind is a necessity for an elder or aged one. This is a point that Paul and Peter would agree on.

Peter told the saints, "Be sober, be vigilant; because your adversary the devil, as a roaring lion, walketh about, seeking whom he may devour" (1 Pet. 5:8). The apostle Peter learned that the devil lies in wait for an opportune time. Peter was writing to make the saints aware of their surroundings, not fearful of them.

Your influence requires that you are aware of what is influencing you and what influences others. Drunkenness impairs your judgment. It distorts your discernment. Drunkenness will position you to make fake friends out of real enemies and fake enemies out of real friends. You can ill afford to let the cheers of the crowd intoxicate you to the point where you get off message and off mission. Stay sober!

How you manage your thirst during celebration time will greatly affect how you navigate the hardship of cross-shaped adversity during the opportune time. If you thirst for affirmation, notoriety, popularity, attention from the opposite sex, influence, or position, you open yourself up to exploitation and manipulation. The will of the crowd is too unstable for you to consume it and be satisfied. You must celebrate, but do so soberly.

Providential Interruption

Intoxication by celebration impedes your ability to rightly discern the times. The writer of Ecclesiastes pens in the third chapter, "To every thing there is a season, and a time to every purpose under the heaven" (Eccles. 3:1). Every time has a purpose. Being sober empowers you to rightly discern the purpose of the time.

The reason why you must be sober during opportune celebrations is because you need to be able to perceive your adversity as providential, not accidental. You will forfeit the advantages of adversity if you can only see the devil's hand in your hardship and not see God's hand in your survival and deliverance.

Cross-shaped adversity may seem like an interruption to your celebration, but it has a sovereign purpose that will lead to even greater celebration. To the intoxicated, Jesus's upcoming hardship would seem like an interruption. However, Jesus, who maintained his sobriety, saw his adversity as purposeful and providential. You must see your opportune celebration the same way. If you see as he sees, eventually you will look like he looks.

You may be wondering, "How do I stay sober or get sobered up?" My answer is to maintain a Christlike perspective. Amid the crowd, the context, the culture, the conflict, and the coming controversy, Jesus stayed focused on his mission! Jesus understood that, regardless of the emotions of the people, the jealousy of the chief priests, the immaturity of the disciples, and the violence of the Romans, he did not come to Jerusalem to celebrate his success; he came to submit himself as a sacrifice. Jesus understood that there was a mission to his misery. There is a purpose to your pain.

Your induction into the fellowship through cross-shaped adversity will be a contradiction of time. It will be the best of times and the worst of times. I encourage you to celebrate your successes, but be sober about your upcoming sacrifices. The same God that formed you for success will also strengthen you for the sacrifice!

YOUR DAY THAT
THE LORD HAS MADE

There is something special about knowing that you are approaching a day that you were made for. Many of you reading this book have had opportunities to bask in the euphoric emotions of events that confirmed that you were in the right place at the right time. The assurance and confidence that comes from knowing that *I am right where God wants me to be* can cause joy to bubble up within us. We love times like those because they feel like destiny.

Our culture in the United States is infatuated with destiny, promise, and purpose. Our relationship with destiny, frankly, can lead to idolatry born of lust because we really do not want destiny for what it does for God or others; we want destiny for what it does for us. Our concept of destiny involves prosperity, material gain, popularity, fame, acclaim, and many other signs of personal wealth, significance, and influence. When we are finally granted access to influential people or platforms, when we grab the mic to sing at the convocation or convention, when we give the acceptance speech at the awards ceremony or the victory address after winning the political office, or when we close the door of our corner office after moving in after a promotion, we often feel the overwhelming emotions of "I was made for this" or "for this cause came I unto this hour" (John 12:27).

Our approach to destiny only gives us a feeling of accomplishment and victory when destiny looks like success. We only feel like "I was made for this" when desired success and opportunity become reality. However, this was not the testimony of Jesus. The cause for which he had come to the earth was not an egocentric opportunity to discuss the kingdom with Caesar or an opportunity to speak to thousands, procure a multimillion-dollar property, or secure a political office through which he could facilitate the business of the kingdom. All these things are great, but Jesus was not made simply for greatness; he was made for *glory*!

In an interesting or ironic twist in John's Gospel, of all the things that Jesus had done in the seven miracles of John, the hour of Jesus's glorification centered on a cross. The cross was the exemplary symbol of humiliation, shame, and suffering. Yet Jesus looked forward to the day of this suffering and said, "for this cause came I unto this hour" (John 12:27); to paraphrase, "I was made for this."

Jesus did not come into the world for a crown. He came to earth for a cross. Jesus remained sober during the celebration because he understood his role in the narrative was not to be the center of celebrated success but the center of the celebration of Passover.

The Passover was centered on the efficacy of a lamb's sacrifice and blood. In just a few days from his entry into the holy city, Jesus would be hoisted on the cross, on a hill called Calvary, for all to see and hear with renewed perspective the words of John the Baptist, "Behold the Lamb of God, which taketh away the sin of the world" (John 1:29).

Nothing sobers a person during a time of celebration like the knowledge of the sacrifice that the celebration requires. The celebration does not negate or exempt you from your responsibilities during the celebration. While the celebration flourishes, there will be sacrifices you have to make.

John Maxwell often shares with the thousands of people who come to hear his talks on leadership, growth, and development that "you have to give up to go up."[1] If your time of celebration happens in a high place like Jerusalem, be aware that if you go up somewhere, you will have to give up something.

I cannot help but imagine what it is like when a candidate for president wins the national election. After all the celebrating and congratulatory felicitations, there has to be an overwhelming sense of responsibility that comes upon the former candidate who will sit in the seat that is heralded as the most powerful in the world. The security briefings, along with the knowledge that your decisions could end lives and that your family will be the target of visceral expectations and scrutiny, you give up your private freedoms to live in a house you did not purchase. You will live most of the moments of your presidency with only two real years to accomplish anything.

While you are celebrating your presidential victory and dancing with colleagues and happy supporters, you know something they do not know. You know that while we celebrate over here, there are others actively plotting your demise and will call it patriotic. It is often no different, unfortunately, in our homes, families, schools, churches, or jobs. It was no different two thousand years ago during the Passover in Jerusalem.

While the city was celebrating what God had done for them, there were some who were actively planning to do something to Jesus. This goes to show that people can celebrate what God has done for them and actively plan to do something to you!

While lifting God up, they are trying to tear you down. I want you to know that "for this cause have you come to this hour." You, like Jesus, were made for this! You were not just made for success; you were made to handle this level of suffering. It is a part of your privilege as a child of God! It's a part of your call! You not only make sacrifices for your success and the success of the people you love; you also make sacrifices that will ultimately benefit the people who plotted against you, denied you, attempted to end your career, sabotaged your influence, and caused your demise. This season of your life is not accidental, but providential. Be encouraged, because you were made for this!

Save Room for Another Cup

During the Passover, it is easier to celebrate and be intoxicated when you are not the lamb! However, when you know you are the lamb, by whose sacrifice the celebration is sponsored, you will sober up and make sure that you leave room for another cup!

"But I say unto you, I will not drink henceforth of this fruit of the vine, until that day when I drink it new with you in my Father's kingdom" (Matt. 26:29). These were the words that Jesus spoke during the supper in the upper room with his disciples. He spoke these words after offering for their consumption the "blood of the new testament," a cup that he told the disciples to "drink ye all of" (Matt. 26:27–28). What the disciples did not understand at the time was that the metaphorical contents of that cup and the means by which it was supplied would be the result of a cup that Jesus would wrestle with the Father to drink. They were able to drink all the cup of the new covenant because Jesus would soon drink all of the bitter cup of sacrifice.

Often, what paves the way to make people better comes at the cost of a leader tasting something bitter. During hardship, what may taste bitter to you may mean better for others. You must make the choice to drink from another cup. You must make that choice soberly. You must understand that you, as a proverbial sacrificial lamb, were made for this!

You may have to sacrifice your right to defend yourself. You may have to sacrifice your right to expose those who accuse you for the liars that they are. You may have to sacrifice your right to demand higher wages than what you are currently receiving. You may have to sacrifice your right be vindictive and unforgiving. You may have to sacrifice your need for validation and affirmation. God knows just what to demand as sacrifice from us to form us into the image of his Son, for to be little Christs is also to be little lambs. God would not place a demand on a person that he or she could not meet. God knows that he made you for this day, and he also made this day for you!

The Day the Lord Has Made

It is impossible to understand the passion narratives, and therefore the advantage of adversity, without revisiting the institution of the feast of the Passover. Thousands of years before the death, burial, and resurrection of Jesus Christ, the prophet and deliverer Moses received a word from the Lord about the Passover. Exodus 12 shares with us the institution of the Passover as a feast and memorial to the newly minted nation of Israel. Moses shared with the congregation the instruction that he received from the Lord about the lamb of sacrifice, what to do with the blood, when to kill the lamb, and many other specifics.

Moses, the messenger of the Lord, only relayed to the people what he had been told by the Lord. This means that the Passover was not an idea that originated with Moses. If Moses was a messenger to the people, then it suffices to say that the Passover celebration did not originate with the people. Additionally, the Egyptians, including their Pharaoh, suffered at the hands of an angel of the Lord at Passover. Obviously, Passover was not Egypt's idea. The idea of Passover was God's idea.

There were no Passovers before the one in Egypt. The innovation and inauguration of this feast was the initiative of God. The Passover was literally a day that the Lord had made. God not only prepared a lamb for the day, but he also prepared the day for the lamb. If it is a day that the Lord hath made, then we should "rejoice and be glad in it" (Ps. 118:24).

We rejoice because of what the day makes visible and what the day makes possible.

When God created the cosmos, the Bible says that he separated light from darkness and that he also made day and night. In our language, we do not have a word that differentiates between day, meaning the time during which it is light, and day, meaning the entirety of twenty-four hours. It is important, for the purposes of this chapter, to consider that there is a part of every twenty-four-hour day that is dark.

Darkness is nestled within every day! Any day that the Lord has made has a space of time within it during which we, his beloved creation, get to see the darkness. The Passover and passion are no different. According to Exodus 12:6, the lamb of the sacrifice was killed during the "evening." This is the same word used to describe the two parts of the day in Genesis—for example, "the evening and the morning were the fourth day" (Gen. 1:19).

The lamb was sacrificed during the evening, when it was getting dark. The lamb was safe in the day, while there was light. It was preserved during the day, separated and protected during the day only because of how it would be used at night. The lamb was prepared in the light for what would happen to it in the dark. God has been preparing you in the light for what will happen to you in the darkness of adversity.

I want you to make sure you understand that when the Bible uses the word *evening*, it is not synonymous with the word *private*. This was not a darkness that could not be seen or be seen in. This darkness was public, and the things that happened in it were public. The Passover sacrifice occurred during the time of day when darkness was exposed.

The provision of the darkness of the day was because the Passover was not just made for the lamb; it was made for another character in the Exodus narrative, a character of whom the writer of Ecclesiastes said there is "a time to be born and a time to die" (Eccles. 3:2). The Passover was a celebration of how God brought the children of Israel out when the destroyer, or death, was allowed into the nation of Egypt for the firstborn one night.

The darkness was not just made for the lamb; it was also made for the destroyer. The blood of the lamb is effective during the time when the destroyer operates. Be not deceived, a destroyer is always lurking in the dark. The Passover was not just the "hour" for which the Lamb of God had come, but it was also the "hour" for the "power of darkness" (Luke 22:53). The Passover was a time of war between the Lamb and the power of darkness.

The textual irony of the passion narratives is startling. Each evangelist disclosed for public consumption and consideration all the things that occurred during the late hours of the night on Thursday and the early hours of the morning Friday, while the sun was down. The writers of the Gospels, literally, shed light on the activities that took place in the dark. The conspirators against Christ wanted to use the cover of natural darkness to conceal the powers of spiritual darkness while destroying Jesus, the light of the world. However, the evangelists would not allow what was done in the dark, by the dark, to stay in the dark. They used the light of the narrative to expose the darkness of the world!

It would be helpful for us to consider what Jesus said about this unique time in his ministry. He said, "When I was daily with you in the temple, ye stretched forth no hands against me: but this is your hour, and the power of darkness" (Luke 22:53). Jesus alluded to the providential nature of the time, suggesting that he understood that this hour was made possible by an allowance of his Father. Yet it was not simply an allowance to execute, but an allowance to expose. Contrary to the belief of the conspirators of the crucifixion, Jesus, through his public execution, was going to make the powers of darkness an open spectacle. As Paul said to the Colossian church, "And having disarmed the powers and authorities, he made a public spectacle of them, triumphing over them by the cross" (Col. 2:15 NIV).

The "hour" of the power of darkness was scheduled by God to expose the darkness for what it is! The light did not come so that we may see in the darkness but so that we might truthfully perceive the darkness! David S. Yeago puts it this way:

> The "hour" when Jesus's enemies seize him to
> carry out their designs upon him is the appointed
> time when God permits the "darkness" to show its
> hand, for the "hour" is always the time appointed
> by God. It is the ascendency of wrong, the domi-
> nating energy of corruption that holds sway over
> the human race, that steps forth to destroy Jesus,
> and thus reveals itself as the one power that lies
> hidden beneath the surface divisions and mutual
> hostilities of human kind. What comes into view
> in the events which devolve around Jesus in the
> last days of his life is nothing less than the whole
> sordid tangle of fear and resentment, shallowness
> and self-deception, confused desire and cold ego-
> tism, that lies hidden like a guilty secret beneath the

> surface of human history, subverting our aspira-
> tions and staining our achievements.[2]

The season of our cross-shaped adversity is not just a time of humiliation, but also of revelation. The "hour" comes so that we may have our discernment calibrated and no longer mistake darkness for something other than darkness. The hour of darkness is, ironically, a time when the darkness cannot hide. The darkness will be exposed and be made a public example. The things that were hidden will come to light.

Your hardship will open your eyes to false friends, hidden agendas, clandestine conspiracies, and so much more. Some of the things you see in the dark will surprise you. Most of what is revealed will disappoint you. God exposes it so that he, by his power, can expel it.

The darkness loves to hide, and it thrives on anonymity and invisibility. A wise man once told me that you cannot take aim at a target while it is in the shadows, but once it is exposed, you can eradicate it. You cannot be delivered from a devil that has not been exposed. The devil, demons, and their ilk dwell in the darkness.

Francis Frangipane, in a wonderful book on the three battlegrounds, shares this insight: "Many Christians debate whether the devil is on the earth or in hell; can he dwell in Christians or only in the world? The fact is, the devil is in darkness. Wherever there is spiritual darkness, there the devil will be."[3] He goes on to argue that this darkness is not restricted to land but is inclusive of mindsets, perspectives, philosophies, emotions, habits, institutions, and more. This means that wherever darkness is, even if it is in the human heart, the devil takes residence there. The hour of darkness is not just a time when the actions of devils and dark men are revealed, but also the intents of their hearts. You cannot continue to grow and mature if you do not have a time when you have seen the darkness.

There Is Deliverance in the Dark

The Passover was a day that the Lord made. The reason why we can rejoice and be glad in it is because of what happened on that day while it was dark. Indeed, the destroyer came when it was dark. The destroyer also passed over the houses of Israel because of a lamb that was slain in the dark.

The Jews celebrated Passover, and we celebrate Jesus's passion because of God's power to deliver us from our destroyer. The deliverance we experience through the lamb's sacrifice happened in the dark. God did not save us or the children of Israel from the dark. He saved us in the dark.

Your adversity will come with some dark moments, agendas, and plans. I want you to take heart, be encouraged, and have hope, because God only allowed the darkness to come so that you may be delivered in it and from it. Your adversity is not just a season of discomfort; it is a season of deliverance. If you make the necessary sacrifices, you too will find that there is deliverance in the darkness.

NOTES

[1] John Maxwell, *The 21 Irrefutable Laws of Leadership: Follow Them and People Will Follow You* (Nashville: Thomas Nelson, 1998).

[2] David S. Yeago, "Introduction," in *The Apostolic Faith: A Catholic and Evangelical Introduction to Christian Theology*, unpublished manuscript (Grand Rapids: Eerdmans, n.d.).

[3] Francis Frangipane, *The Three Battlegrounds* (Cedar Rapids: Arrow Publications, 1989).

YOUR PRAYERS AND
THE GARDEN

The gospel of Jesus Christ must be told and taught. We preach and study it because the story of Jesus's teaching demands telling. When I use the word *teaching*, I do not mean it in just the active sense of the term. There is more to the gospel of Jesus Christ than just the lessons he taught in parables. The entire narratives are lessons. Jesus taught using methods, messages, and modeling.

One of the key concepts Jesus taught by message and method was the discipline of prayer. Each of the synoptic Gospels have extensive references to Jesus going away to a quiet or reclusive place to pray. John's Gospel contains the priestly prayer in the Garden, which is the longest prayer of Jesus contained in Scripture. You cannot read the gospel and not learn that Jesus was a man of prayer and desired for his followers to be people of prayer.

Jesus employed an interesting method to teach the importance of prayer. He taught on the subject in Matthew 6 and Luke 11. The disciples would often watch Jesus steal away and come back from prayer operating in phenomenal power. The disciples knew, by example, the power of private and personal prayer. Ironically, they learned this lesson by direct observation of the power and indirect knowledge of prayer. They knew Jesus prayed. They knew prayer led to power. They did not know what Jesus prayed or how Jesus prayed.

Luke's Gospel shares several times when Jesus prayed. After watching Jesus come back from prayer walking in power time after time after time, the disciples entreated Jesus by saying, "Lord, teach us to pray" (Luke 11:1). Jesus prayed so privately and intimately that the disciples were curious about what he said during his prayers. The privacy of his prayers intrigued them. They wanted the power but did not know how to pray.

If you are anything like me, you have had that same struggle. You know that prayer is the key to walking in Christlike power. You know to schedule time in a secret place to pray. What baffles you about your prayer life may be the fact that even though you know when to pray and where to pray, you do not know what to pray. The disciples knew that frustration all too well.

Jesus taught his disciples to pray the model prayer in Luke 11 and Matthew 6. "Our Father which art in Heaven, Hallowed be thy name. Thy kingdom come, Thy will be done in earth, as it is in heaven. Give us this day our daily bread. And forgive us our debts, as we forgive our debtors. And lead us not into temptation, but deliver us from evil: For thine is the kingdom, and the power, and the glory, for ever. Amen" (Matt. 6:9–14).

Can you imagine the disconnect for the disciples when they heard this lesson? They knew Jesus to be a man who could pray all night long. Surely, he was saying more than this short prayer. There had to be more to it than that! After all the excitement to hear Jesus's lesson on prayer, there was still much to be desired after the lesson was over. If I were one of the disciples, I would want to actually be in a private place and be close enough to see Jesus and hear him while he prayed.

What the disciples did not know is that, on the night before the Passover, they would get their chance to see and hear Jesus pray. Unfortunately, the power of the lesson would expose their weaknesses and be the best and worst night to learn how to pray.

In the Garden of Gethsemane, the disciples got their final lesson on prayer. Jesus would not just expose them to the method or message of prayer, but the model of prayer. "Father, if thou be willing, remove this cup from me: nevertheless not my will, but thine, be done" (Luke 22:42).

The power of the prayer of Christ in the Garden of Gethsemane involved the intense pressure of the context of the prayer. Before we explore the power of the context of this prayer, let's first examine the content of the prayer to see what lessons we can learn from Jesus.

The words Jesus spoke in the Garden prayers of Matthew and Luke are veiled within the model prayer Jesus taught his disciples to pray in Matthew 6 and Luke 11. Jesus said, "Father, if thou be willing, remove this cup from me: nevertheless not my will, but thine, be done" (Luke 22:42). At the center of this prayer of our Lord is the sovereignty of God the Father and the will of the Father in heaven being done on earth. In this Garden prayer, Jesus prayed the model prayer and showed us how the will of heaven gets done on earth!

Our Father which art in heaven, Hallowed be thy name

The Garden prayer starts off with the word *Father*, the same Father the model prayer is addressed to. Jesus, in the Garden with his disciples, was not talking to any of them. There was no one else to talk to other than his Father, who was not in the Garden, but in heaven. Jesus, the Father's Son, had such reverence for his Father that even though he knew his Father's proper name, he did not address him as such. Jesus knew that the name of the Father was too holy to be uttered by human lips, so he exemplified reverence by not saying his Father's name.

Thy kingdom come

The coming of the kingdom is implicit in the Garden prayer of Jesus because the kingdom is present in its king. Jesus is the kingdom and has come into the earth. The kingdom coming to earth is represented in Jesus's advent to earth. Jesus prayed for the kingdom to come and preached that the kingdom has come. He was the answer to his own prayers and the subject of his own preaching.

Thy will be done in earth, as it is in heaven

The kingdom comes to do the will of the Father on the earth. Jesus shows us the strategy for the accomplishment of the will of the kingdom on earth. The strategy for successful completion of the will of the kingdom on earth is not explicitly stated in the model prayer but is explicitly modeled in the Garden prayer. The will of the king and his kingdom is accomplished by submission. Andy Crouch, in his book *Culture Making*, alludes to the uncanny way the passion of Jesus Christ was his greatest accomplishment.[1] Jesus's greatest accomplishment was achieved by what was done to him, not by what he himself did. The will of the Father is accomplished through active trust. We act in accordance with the will of the Father through submission with powerful trust. The strongest act of a son occurs when he actively trusts in and submits to his father.

Give us this day our daily bread

As we discussed in an earlier chapter, the day of this prayer is the day that the Lord made and a day that the Lord Jesus was made for. Jesus, according to his own theology of the Last Supper, is the bread that is broken. He was not only the bread given on that day, but he was also the historical manna that sustained the children of Israel in the wilderness. This world is our wilderness! We only survive because of the bread that is given to us daily, which is the bread that was given for us on Good Friday. Jesus is the bread given to us. Jesus is the bread given for us.

Forgive us our debts, as we forgive our debtors

Since Jesus has become our bread and sacrifice, we can now be forgiven and forgive. The Lord's Prayer is only possible to be uttered because of the person and work of Jesus Christ. This phase is an image of the horizontal and vertical beams of our Lord's cross. He was crucified to bring reconciliation between God and man (vertical) and between man and man (horizontal).

God forgiving us as we forgive others alludes to relationship between the beams of the cross. One beam hinges on the other. Jesus would soon hang on the vertical beam as his feet were on the earth and his eyes were on the heavens. He would also hang on the horizontal beam, as his hands reached out to sinful humanity. He hanged there suspended in the air, both as priest and sacrifice, reconciling the world to God and each other.

Lead us not into temptation

The cross of Jesus Christ seals for us a relationship with a God who is faithful and just to forgive us our sins. As forgiven citizens of the king, we can now follow his lead. The power of his cross makes us reflect on our weaknesses. We can see ourselves in the light of this cross more clearly, knowing, as the children of Israel learned in the Old Testament, that we do not want to get to the edge of the promised land and not get in because we fell to the temptation of the wilderness.

We know the story of our crucified Lord. He was led into the wilderness to be tempted so that he could accomplish what Israel in the wilderness could not. We understand our frailty, so we pray that God not lead us, his forgiven sons and daughters, where he led his only begotten Son. We are aware that there are some temptations that we are not strong enough to withstand. During Jesus's anguish in the Garden of Gethsemane, he said these words to the disciples who followed him to the Garden that night: "Pray that ye enter not into temptation" (Luke 22:40).

Deliver us from evil

We, by faith, can be delivered from evil because of the one who was delivered to evil! Jesus was delivered into the hands of sinful men by the betrayal of Judas so that we might be delivered from evil and the evil one. Our deliverance causes us to ascend from our shackles, but his deliverance caused him to descend into hell. The cry for deliverance from evil recalls Israel's history in Egypt and the cry of an enslaved family who, by the nine plagues and the blood of a lamb, were delivered from evil. Jesus, who is the Lamb of God and a prophet like Moses, is our deliverer and our deliverance!

For thine is the kingdom, and the power, and the glory

The pain of Jesus's process led to a plentiful possession. Satan offered Jesus kingdoms and the glory thereof. Jesus refused his offer because of the one kingdom of all kingdoms, the kingdom of God. This kingdom is not the devil's to give. The phrase "thine is the kingdom" exclaims that this kingdom is in the Father's possession. Jesus tells us here that it is in the Father's possession to give, and in Luke, Jesus declares that it is also the Father's pleasure to give unto us the kingdom (Luke 12:32).

By the end of Matthew, the kingdom, the power, and the glory belong to Jesus. He said that all power in heaven and earth has been given to him. This clause of the prayer alludes to the power of the resurrection and the second coming of our Lord Jesus. It implies that if we endure with patience our deliverance from evil, we, like Jesus, will be rewarded with authority and glory. The Father delivers us from evil because he, by the resurrection, delivered his Son from evil and gave him all authority in heaven and on earth. This kingdom will have no end—forever and ever amen!

The model prayer of Jesus is literally the Lord's Prayer because the entirety of the prayer is about our Lord. The prayer taught by the Son speaks of the Father and the coming of the kingdom on the earth, which is Jesus's birth. The prayer speaks of the will of the Father being done, which is Jesus's betrayal, trial, humiliation, and death. The daily bread, forgiveness, and deliverance scream of the Lord's cross, which is how forgiveness and deliverance were secured. The last clause speaks to the resurrection and victorious coming of our Lord in the last day.

When Jesus taught the disciples this prayer, he was teaching them how to pray the gospel. Jesus, in the Garden of Gethsemane, consummated the lesson by showing the disciples that praying in the spirit of the model prayer is easier taught than done.

Easier Said than Done

In Philippians 2:6–11, there is a curious pericope that many consider an early Christ hymn. It is believed to be so because the hymns of the ancient church seemed to follow a pattern: preexistence of Christ, humiliation of Christ, and exaltation of Christ.[2] Their songs were not just to him but about him. Christ hymns were more than praise; they were doctrine.

The hymn says, "Who, being in the form of God, thought it not robbery to be equal with God: But made himself of no reputation, and took upon him the form of a servant, and was made in the likeness of men" (Phil. 2:6–7). The text shares with us a powerful revelation by using the terminology of Genesis. When it says, "made in the likeness of men," it is indicative of the Fall. Man was created in the likeness of God, but because of the Fall, humanity no longer bears God's likeness as it once did. Humanity, because of the fall, now has its own likeness that differs from the image and likeness of God, which was originally given to humanity according to Genesis 1:26. Jesus, for us and our salvation, took on the likeness of men so that we might be restored to the likeness of God.

The great patristics put it this way: "He became like us, so that we could become like Him!" Nestled within these words is the idea of kenosis, in which Jesus is said to make himself of no reputation. Another translation says he "emptied himself" (Phil. 2:7 NRSV). Kenosis is the technical term for this self-emptying of Jesus. The King James Version says he made himself of no reputation. The Son of God who "thought it not robbery to be equal with God" (Phil. 2:6) emptied himself of his reputation as God.

He did not empty himself into the form and likeness of men; he emptied himself in order to take on the form of a servant. Kenosis is how he went from the form of God to the form of a servant. To take on that form, he had to empty himself of his omnipotence, omnipresence, and omniscience. Jesus did not have all power when he came to the earth; he was limited because of his form.

Jesus took on the form of humanity, with all its limitations, temptations, passions, and proclivities. What made him different was the fact that Jesus was not only the son of a human mother, but also the Son of the heavenly Father.

When Jesus worked miracles on earth, he did so as fully human and fully God. His ministry not only showed us what is possible for God, but what is possible for a man who is filled with God. When he healed the sick, he did it as God and man. When he revealed the events of the end times, he did it as God and man. When he calmed the raging sea, he did it as God and man. When he walked on water, he did it as God and man. All these things he did in the form of a servant!

Adam, however, never walked in that measure of power. So how did taking on the form of a servant in the likeness of men cause Jesus to know what it is like to be Adam?

The Gospels reveal Jesus's humanity by disclosing episodes in the narrative when he experienced the limitations of the flesh. Jesus visited a well in Samaria because he was thirsty. Jesus got hungry during the forty-day fast in the wilderness. He was tempted at all points just as we are, yet was without sin.

All these things Adam had before the Fall. Adam had an appetite before the Fall. Adam was tempted before the Fall. Adam was mandated to dress and keep the Garden, which means he had work to do before the Fall. How was Jesus, the last Adam, like the first Adam? How did he know what it is like to be under the curse of sin even though he didn't sin?

To answer this question, we must examine the first three chapters of Genesis in tandem with this pericope in Luke 22 to find out what they share. On the surface, we will find that both Adam and Jesus were in a garden. Adam was in the Garden of Eden, or paradise. Jesus was in the Garden of Gethsemane, or the place of pressing. However, this does not satisfy our inquiry. When we examine Genesis 3:19, we find a clue to help us. Genesis 3:19 contains a prophetic prognostication given to Adam. God told him that, because of his sin, "In the sweat of thy face shalt thou eat bread."

We find Jesus in Luke 22:44 doing something that no other Gospel says he did. Nowhere in the gospel narratives other than this verse is it recorded that Jesus sweat! What makes this sweat like the sweat of Genesis 3:19 is not the experience but the reason of his sweating. The curse of Adam was to sweat not because of heat or exercise, but work! God said that in the sweat of your face shall you eat bread (Gen. 3:19). Bread is not a natural phenomenon; it is a cultural phenomenon. The earth does not make bread; the earth makes wheat. Men make bread.

Adam would sweat from doing the work he was supposed to do. He was mandated to make something of the world, and, because of the Fall, he would have to sweat while doing his work. He would have to lose his life to sustain life. In the Garden of Gethsemane, the last Adam who was sent to the world for what he could make of the world was sweating in a garden not because of his worries but because of his work.

The sweating of the Lord Jesus in the Garden accurately depicts the extreme intensity of the pressure he was under on the night he was betrayed. The cup from which he was to drink contained enough calamity and chaos that even Christ Jesus prayed, "Father, if thou be willing, remove this cup from me" (Luke 22:42). The work he was called to do, after seeing crowds of people and having the fame of his name proclaimed throughout the country, now had him alone in the Garden praying that "this cup" be removed.

Some adversity, the kind shaped like crosses, come with our own garden experience. Jesus's Gethsemane experience left him lonely because of his exceptionalism. Jesus was in intense prayer because what he was being asked to do could only be done by him.

Your exceptionalism will create a separation between you and others. Because you can do things no one else can do, you will be asked to perform tasks no one else can perform. There is a grave cost to being able to do things that no one else can do. The name of the reward of exceptionalism is authority. The name of the cost of exceptionalism is responsibility!

To walk in an authority everybody wants, you must carry responsibility no one wants. If you are exceptional in any area of your life, please be aware that your exceptionalism may reward you with unprecedented success, but it also requires that you make unprecedented sacrifices.

No one else could make this sacrifice or be this sacrifice for sin except Jesus. In the Garden, Jesus showed us that sonship and fellowship will require of you an exceptional sacrifice. Jesus could not delegate this work to anyone else. This cup could not pass.

His exceptionalism made him eligible to do more than the difficult; he could do the impossible. What was impossible for others was possible, yet difficult, for him! This work would not be easy, and your work, no matter how gifted and exceptional you are, is not going to be easy either.

I do not want to be the bearer of bad news, but your real work is going to make you sweat! It is not going to be difficult because of the pain you cause yourself, but it is going to be challenging because of the pain that will be caused by others. Praying "thy will be done" is much easier on the mountain than it is in the garden, because in the garden, the will includes an active decision to allow others to cause you harm.

Our exceptionalism makes us authoritative and responsible, but it also makes us targets. When you are a leader and become a target, the only place for people to attack you is your back. Induction to the fellowship often comes by being betrayed and denied by those who you once thought had your back. The pain of knowing you will soon be betrayed into the hands of people who do not mean you well by a person you thought meant you well puts your exceptional restraint and exceptional love on trial.

The prayer "Thy will be done in earth, as it is in heaven" (Matt. 6:10) is not a request but a confession of surrender. Jesus taught it on the mountain but modeled it in the Garden. Teaching others is one thing; modeling it is totally different. Your hardship will require you to model what you have taught your followers. I can tell you from experience that modeling your teaching is easier said than done! The classroom is a much easier place to surrender than Gethsemane!

Our level of success is commensurate with our level of surrender! The pressure of surrender is tremendous, especially when the Father is negotiating the terms. Most of us, like Jesus, will have no problem resisting the devil when he offers us kingdoms. However, we will have a problem trusting and submitting to the Father when he offers us a cross. "Get thee behind me, Satan" (Matt. 16:23) is easier to say than "nevertheless not my will, but thine, be done" (Luke 22:42). Repeatedly praying that phrase is enough to make you sweat.

The I's Have It!

During this episode of the passion of Jesus Christ, he experienced a unique type of loneliness. The gospel narratives all share with us that Jesus was not by himself in the Garden, and this is what made his loneliness unique. He had company, but no companions. He would go through the next phase of his tenure on earth alone. He was alone because no one else but him could be crucified for humanity. He was alone because he was the only one in his company who had any knowledge of what was about to transpire over the next few hours and days. He was alone because that was a burden he carried for people, not with people, even though he would carry it in front of people.

The kind of loneliness Jesus was undergoing can only be described by the words of Matthew and Mark in their renditions of the Garden narratives. Both Gospels use a phrase to indicate how Jesus distanced himself when he went to pray in the Garden: "And he went a little farther" (Matt. 26:39); "And he went forward a little" (Mark 14:35). Jesus intentionally separated himself from the rest of his disciples to engage in a conversation with his Father about his future. The loneliness of Christ was both purposeful and intentional!

Cross-shaped adversity will require you to go a little farther than others. The first word that comes to mind because of that phrase is *extreme*, and the second is *extra*. Growing into the person of Christ or conforming to the image of our king will come under some extreme circumstances and feel very "extra."

When you feel like you have suffered enough, you may experience some extra suffering. When you feel like you have undergone enough stress, you will experience some extra stress. When you have had your fill of people talking about you, making Facebook Live videos about you, criticizing you on all social media platforms, and misconstruing your intentions and motivations, then things will go a little farther, and you will experience the extreme of extra suffering.

The temple cadre were about to do extra things to Jesus— extra trials, extra mocking, extra accusations. Peter denied Jesus three times, as if once were not enough. The Roman soldiers were going to do extra things to Jesus's body. Scourging him was enough for Pilate, but not enough for the mob. There will be times when you feel like you have had enough, and God himself will allow you to go through a little extra!

Going a little farther, experiencing the pain of extra, is the cost of being extraordinary. Could it be possible that the extra circumstances of your life are forming you into an extraordinary person? Extraordinary pain, not extraordinary privilege, makes extraordinary people. Jesus was not ordinary, and neither are you.

Jesus, knowing that things were about to go a little farther than normal in pain, prefaced the process by going a little farther in prayer. Our extraordinary process requires that you and I go a little bit farther in prayer. While our companions are asleep, we must go a little bit farther in prayer.

You see, going a little farther implies a comparison. Extraordinary implies a comparison. Jesus's going a little farther implies that the disciples had gone as far as they could go. Jesus was alone because his extraordinary circumstances and purpose required that he leave the disciples. Jesus's isolation was the result of his voluntary separation. He was not left behind; he left them behind.

There comes a point in our maturation when God begins to distinguish us from others. God's intention is not to isolate you, but to separate you. God wants you to stay in community but to understand that you are not common. To make the distinction between you and the people around you, God brings about a scenario in which the people in your circle go as far as they can, and then he calls you a little farther.

God orchestrated a similar scenario in Exodus 24, when he called Moses and others to come up to him on the mountain, but then he said to Moses, "And Moses alone shall come near the LORD" (Exod. 24:2). God commanded Moses to bring Aaron, Nadab, Abihu, and the seventy elders of Israel up to the mountain, but they were to "worship ye afar off" (Exod. 24:1), while "Moses alone shall come near." God commanded Moses to bring his circle of influencers as far as they could go, and then he called Moses to go a little farther.

Your hardship will put pressure on existing relationships. You will experience the pain and privilege of being extraordinarily distinct from others. In other words, you will go as far as you can with your circle, and then you must go a little farther. Jesus, at this point in his life, had taken the twelve as far as they could go. He went a little farther in prayer, and the remaining eleven went fast to sleep.

My father once taught me a short poem that he accredited to the great patristic, Augustine, the bishop of Hippo. I later discovered that it was a stanza from a poem called *The Ladder of St. Augustine.*

> The heights that great men have reached and kept
> were not reached in sudden flight. But they while
> their companions slept toiled upward in the night.[3]

Quoting this poem for years and believing that it was accredited to Augustine did not cause me to consider that the poet may have been talking about Jesus. Jesus was a great man who reached a great height, and in the Garden, we see him, while his companions slept, toil upward in the night. The sleeping disciples are key to establishing your distinction and refining your discernment!

As we look at the Garden prayer narrative, we see that Jesus did not tell everyone in his circle where he would be, and neither did he tell everyone in his inner circle how he was feeling. Jesus made distinctions between these groups because he chose them for reasons that many of them would not discover until after his ascension. The crowd at the mountain was not the same as the circle in the Garden. You must understand that you cannot take everybody to the garden. You must also understand that not taking everybody to the garden does not mean you cannot take anybody. The garden is reserved for your inner circle. There's no room in your secret place for the crowd you lead in a public space.

Your inner circle can go farther than the crowd, even though they cannot go as far as you can. Going to the garden for prayer will always boil down and distill your circle. The garden is the place where you distinguish between those who can support your work and those who can support your worries. The questions are: Who is in your inner circle? Whom can you trust to support you in your work while knowing your worries? Whom can you ask to pray for an hour when your hour has come? Who can you tell, "My soul is exceeding sorrowful" (Mark 14:34)? Who are your insulators, intercessors, and insiders?

Who Are Your Insulators?

Did you know that Goliath was not the only giant David confronted? In 2 Samuel 21:16, there is a brief narrative about a giant named Ishbibenob, who thought to kill King David.

Ishbibenob did not die by the end of David's sword but at the hands of Abishai, one of David's men. After killing this giant, the men of Israel told their king that he would no longer go with them to battle so that "thou quench not the light of Israel" (2 Sam. 21:17). Not every giant you face do you have enough flame to fight. There is a giant you will face that you will need insulators to protect you from.

Jesus's own words tell us that he is the light of the world and that we are the light of the world. When Jesus spoke those words, there was no electricity. The lights of his day were powered by oil and wicks. To maintain the vibrance of a light in Jesus's day you had to keep oil in your lamp and keep your wick trimmed. The fire of the lamp consumed the wick, diminishing its power to provide light long-term. Your light will have seasons when it grows dim. You will need men like those in David's army to provide a shield so your light does not go out. You need insulation.

Insulators function as a line of protection and defense from the elements and environments that threaten your light. Let's be honest, there are times when our light grows dim. There are circumstances and situations that, instead of fanning and fueling our flame, extinguish it. No matter how hard you try, you cannot protect your own flame from every adversary. You need insulators.

As the men of David provided insulation for the "light of Israel," and as the priest trimmed the golden lampstand in the temple, the twelve provided insulation for the Lord Jesus Christ. They provided a buffer between the light of the world and the darkness. They provided insulation so that the cold of the world did not overwhelm the warmth provided by the light of the world.

You need people in your life who can keep you from going dark and growing cold. You need people in your inner circle who can provide protection, not with their prowess but, at a minimum, with their presence.

During the earthly ministry of Christ, there were few places Jesus went that the twelve did not follow. The twelve were so eager to insulate Jesus that they tried to keep children away from him and tried to ignore a Canaanite woman whose daughter needed deliverance from a devil.

Insulators facilitate access to your fire and flame. They help determine what gets to you. They also have a quality in which they can take the cold of the outer circle without compromising the heat of the inner circle. Their presence does not zap your energy and enthusiasm; it helps maintain it.

Here is one more thing about insulators that you must understand: every one of the twelve were insulators, including Judas. Judas compromised his role as an insulator and was used to allow the darkness in. The role of Judas, though purposeful, was painful. The cost of your cross will expose faults in some of your insulators.

Who Are Your Intercessors?

In each of the gospel narratives about the passion of the Lord Jesus, one disciple is absent from the Garden episode: Judas Iscariot. The twelve, as they were called throughout most of the gospel story, became the eleven. These eleven men received instruction from Jesus at the Garden to do three things: sit there, watch, and pray that they enter not into temptation (Matt. 26:36, 38, 41). Their position, posture, and prayers made them intercessors. The absence of Judas at the time of Jesus's commands to sit, watch, and pray suggests that not all insulators are intercessors and that all intercessors are insulators. Judas's insulation was only executed by his presence and absence. The other eleven were about to execute their intercessory responsibilities through their position, posture, and prayers.

When Jesus arrived at the Garden, he told the eleven to "sit ye here" (Mark 14:32). Jesus gave these men a post, or position. The intercessors in your inner circle must have a post they are aware of. They must know their place in your life. Jesus's request implied that the place of their post was as far as they could go. Your intercessors need to know how far they can go with you. Some of your intercessors may only have a relationship post, or a financial post, or a health post. Whatever post you designate needs to be clear so they know what area of your life they are supposed to be on watch and pray for.

Sitting is not a sleeping posture; lying down is a sleeping posture. Your intercessors must balance sitting at their post in a resting position with sitting at their post in a ready position! Sitting establishes their presence in a particular place without creating unnecessary alarm, but it also provides them with enough perspective to see things close to the ground and high in the sky. Intercessors must be close enough to see you but far away enough to see impending danger on the horizon. They must also be balanced enough to create calm, not anxiety, by their presence. My pastoral care professor called it being an N.A.P.—a non-anxious presence. Unfortunately, the disciples took literal naps instead of being N.A.P.s.

They were told to sit in a particular place and watch. Jesus understood that he did not have enough eyes to watch out for himself. You don't either. You need some people in your life who can be on watch for you. Who do you have in your life who is positioned close enough to you who can look out for you? Accountability partners look within, and intercessors must be on the lookout. They sit, rested and ready, but they also watch.

The word *watch* has several different uses. *Watch* can be a verb, it can be a word for a device that tells time, or it can be a military term used to identify a shift in which a soldier has to look out for enemies during the night. The text suggests that Jesus wanted the disciples to keep watch, to look out for impending danger or adversaries. I would like to suggest that intercessors posture themselves according to all three of the uses of the word *watch*.

Your intercessors cannot fulfill the responsibilities of their watch if they do not have a watch that tells them when to watch. Intercessors need to know the times and seasons they are needed most so they can stay on their posts. They cannot be left in the dark to wonder when you need to be watched or watched out for. Do not leave them in the dark when things get dark.

Suffering lasts for set seasons. Your pain will only be at an unbearable intensity for a set time. Your intercessors need indicators of when you anticipate that time coming so they can be on the lookout for behaviors and habits that will keep you from your future and create contexts for you to fall or fail. Your intercessors need to be able to discern the times, but they will benefit from you disclosing the times in your life when they need to be on watch.

The power of your intercessors is expressed through the prayers they utter while they are in a watchful posture sitting at the ready post. Intercessors are postured between you and danger so nothing gets in between you and God. Cross-shaped adversity will demand a lot, if not all, of your attention. Intercessors provide prayerful watch for dangerous distractions that try to keep you from destiny.

Jesus, in his wisdom, did something uncanny in Luke's Gospel. He asked his disciples to pray that they enter not into temptation. The phrase "enter not into temptation" is extremely close to the prayer that Jesus taught them to pray in Luke 11: "lead us not into temptation." Jesus asked them to pray according to how they had been taught to do so. Do not ask for someone's prayers if you do not know how they have been taught to pray.

By this point in Jesus's ministry, the disciples had seen him pray and walk in power enough that they asked for teaching on prayer. However, in this episode in Jesus's ministry, they were being asked to pray according to the teaching they desired and received. Your intercessors must want to learn how to pray and be taught how to do the same.

Interestingly, they were asked to pray for themselves. We often think that intercessors are those who pray for others and on another's behalf. The eleven were asked to sit there and watch out for Jesus but to pray for themselves. They were asked to pray for themselves so they could perform the tasks Jesus asked them to do. They were praying so they could faithfully sit and watch. You must understand that the pressure you are under will put pressure on your close relationships. This pressure will make what was once easy to do naturally, difficult to do without the supernatural. Your intercessors are going to need to be "prayed up" to sit and watch the things that will unfold during your hardship. The temptation of the garden is to allow worry to make them weary enough to stop watching! They must pray, "lead us not into temptation."

Who Are Your Insiders?

In Mark's Gospel, there is a distinction made within the ranks of the eleven as they watched with Jesus in the Garden of Gethsemane. Mark tells us, in chapter 14, that after he told the eleven to "Sit ye here, while I shall pray" (Mark 14:32), he "taketh with him Peter and James and John, and began to be sore amazed, and to be very heavy; And saith unto them, My soul is exceeding sorrowful unto death: tarry ye here, and watch" (Mark 14:33–34). Yikes!

Can you imagine the overwhelming sense of danger these three disciples felt when they heard these words? They had seen Jesus raise a little girl from the dead. They had seen Jesus be transfigured. Peter experienced walking on water at the words of Jesus. After witnessing that magnitude of power, seemingly out of nowhere, Jesus exposed them to his inner pain.

Jesus separated these three from the rest of the eleven. Jesus had insiders within his inner circle—twelve insulators, eleven intercessors, but only three insiders.

Peter, James, and John, the insiders, saw Jesus in two extremes. They saw him reveal himself in an extremely divine form during the transfiguration. They now saw him in an extremely vulnerable expression in the Garden of Gethsemane. Notice the numbers, and learn from them. You will have more insulators than intercessors, and you will have fewer insiders than you do insulators or intercessors. Only a few people can handle your extremes.

Truly gifted people have extremes. We can be extremely disciplined and extremely indulgent. We can be extremely excited and extremely discouraged. We have the potential to reach high highs as well as low lows. We may not practice both extremes, but within, we know that the potential to be extreme is always there. Some of the highs we reach are because of our charisma, confidence, or competence. Our lows, however, are often circumstantial. You cannot expose the entirety of your inner circle to your highs and your lows because many of them cannot handle it.

I want to make sure I am clear here, so bear with me. As a son or daughter of God, you possess his Spirit internally. There is divinity in you! However, you are still human. Your maturation into Christlikeness is often coupled with experiencing extremes between your inner divinity and humanity. You can operate in great power, but that power does not exempt you from experiencing great pain. In many cases, the height of your success is coupled with deep suffering. The depth of your suffering is much like Jesus disclosed that day. The pressure of his purpose made him "exceeding sorrowful unto death" (Mark 14:34). You must admit that there are times when you, too, become "sore amazed" and "very heavy" (Mark 14:33).

Your gifts, talents, ambition, successes, and acclaim do not seem to be enough to insulate you from circumstantial or purposeful suffering. No matter what others think, you are not superman or superwoman. For this reason, you must be careful who you allow to see you when your "cape" is off. Please hear me clearly—not everyone can handle the vulnerability of your humanity!

Jesus never sinned, so exposing the three to the depths of his humanity had nothing to do with sin. Jesus was careful not to show the other eleven the depth of his soul's sorrow. It is not the sins of the flesh that people cannot handle; it's the sorrow of your soul! Who can you tell, "My soul is exceeding sorrowful unto death"? Take it from me, you need insiders.

Do not make the mistake of telling insulators and intercessors inside information. I have made that mistake and paid for it dearly. Exposing the wrong people to inside information will create more sorrow for you than the circumstances call for. If you expose the sorrow of your soul to those who are not built for it, you will feel disappointed in yourself when they abandon you. Make sure that the people you have identified as insiders are up for the job.

There is only one factor to consider when discerning who to designate as an insider. Discerning your insiders requires that you answer the following question: What role does this person play in the future? You identify insiders and designate them as such now because you have prayerfully discerned who they will become later. Consider that Jesus told Peter that he was exceedingly sorrowful after telling Peter that he would deny him three times. Peter was an insider because of his future role in the church, not because he was the perfect disciple.

Peter, James, and John all played prominent roles among the disciples after the resurrection of Jesus. Jesus knew their futures and exposed them to the extremes of his divinity and humanity only because of the role they would play in the days to come. Your friendships and fellowships should be developed based on the future, not the past.

Exposing your insiders to your humanity will help them in the future to better handle theirs. You cannot handle the privilege of pain without exposing a few insiders to privileged information.

NOTES

[1] Andy Crouch, *Culture Making: Recovering Our Creative Calling* (Downers Grove: InterVarsity Press, 2008).

[2] Marg Mowczko, "The Creed (Hymn) of Philippians 2:6–11," *Marg Mowczko* blog, May 1, 2010, accessed February 5, 2022, https://margmowczko.com/the-creed-of-philippians-2/.

[3] Henry Wadsworth Longfellow, *The Complete Poetical Works of Henry Wadsworth Longfellow* (Redditch, UK: Read Books Ltd., 2013).

YOUR ADVERSARIES
ALL AROUND

Cross-shaped adversity comes with cross-shaped adversaries. The vertical beam of the cross represents conflict with spiritual forces from the darkness. The horizontal beam of cross-shaped adversity represents the conflict you experience with human adversaries. You cannot handle adversity like Christ if you do not have a Christlike perspective of your adversaries.

It is obvious from the gospel narratives that Jesus was well aware of his adversaries and their purposes and powers. Jesus knew about the plot against him and how it involved Judas, the chief priest, and the elders of Israel. Jesus's conversation with Pilate, in John 19, gives implicit evidence that Jesus also knew the role Pilate played in his passion.

I believe Jesus's perspective was formed and informed by a little discussed fact. That fact is that the entire gospel of Jesus Christ develops and unfolds as a story. Stories have authors, heroes, villains, antagonists, protagonists, plots, subplots, climaxes, and happy endings. As a matter of fact, the written Gospels are classified as narrative biographies. God authored the gospel, Jesus lived it, and the Holy Ghost inspired Matthew, Mark, Luke, and John to write it.

You too have a biography. You have a story, one that is authored by God. Psalm 139:16 (NIV) says, "Your eyes saw my unformed body; all the days ordained for me were written in your book before one of them came to be." Your adversity and your adversaries are a part of your story, but not the entirety of your story. If you can understand this, then you can manage your adversity like Christ because you understand the roles you and your adversaries play in your biography.

Know Your Role

The role you play in your biographical narrative is the hero. Heroes accomplish the impossible by overcoming what seems to be insurmountable. Heroes, in both secular and sacred literature, are champions of overwhelming challenges. This means that your life's challenges are opportunities for you to exhibit heroic character.

A survey and study of Scripture will show you that the main characters of the Bible were known for heroic feats. Noah building the ark, Samson slaying a thousand men with the jawbone of a donkey, David defeating Goliath, Daniel persevering in the lion's den, and Esther rescuing God's people from extinction in Persia are all stories of heroes overcoming challenges. However, in many of the stories I have named, none of the heroes, though facing impossible challenges, were wounded and scarred while accomplishing the impossible.

The story of the suffering servant in Isaiah presents a different motif for biblical heroes. The story of the suffering servant is the prophetic precursor for the story of the gospel of Jesus Christ. Jesus's story, which is the greatest story ever told, does not have a hero who "cannot be touched with the feeling of our infirmities" (Heb. 4:15). Whereas the other heroes in the Old Testament had flaws but seemed to overcome challenges without a scratch on them, Jesus was flawless and was "wounded for our transgressions" (Isa. 53:5). Even after his resurrection, Jesus still had the scars of his wounds.

I remember a time in prayer when God and I were conversing about my holy hardship. I wanted to know why things had to be so difficult. I asked God, "Why do things have to be so hard? Why can't things go smoothly and easier for me? I'm trying to live to please you and it seems like the way of the transgressor is hard, but the way of the godly is so much harder!"

After the Lord allowed me to vent and finish my tantrum, he told me to review the closing scenes of my favorite movies. Of course, he knows I like all of the superhero movies: *Superman*, *The Avengers*, *Thor*, *Iron Man*, and *Captain America*. I am also fond of the *Transformers*, *Fast and Furious*, *John Wick* (forgive me), and the *Mission: Impossible* franchise. What I discovered as I recalled the climactic scene of those movies was a pattern. In all the movies I love, the climactic scene has a hero who is bruised, battered, wounded, and scarred, but triumphant.

The kind of biographies God writes for his sons and daughters are stories of heroic journeys in which they overcome the odds and ultimately triumph, but not without being wounded and bruised. Just look at the book of Acts and you will see the pattern of the gospel of Jesus Christ within the lives of the early apostles. Peter and John were flogged, the church was persecuted, and Paul was stoned and shipwrecked. By the end of the book of Acts, all the heroic characters were triumphant, but bruised. Your role as the hero in your story will be no different.

You will overcome the odds. You will ultimately triumph. However, you will still experience being wounded and bruised. Here is the good news: just as Jesus's wounds ultimately healed, so will yours. Isaiah writes, "with his stripes we are healed" (Isa. 53:5). The wounds Jesus endured unlocked healing for others. His wounds healed, and we are healed by his wounds. The story of your life as you are inducted into this fellowship of his suffering will also end with your wounds healing and healing others. As Revelation says, "And they overcame him by the blood of the Lamb, and by the word of their testimony" (Rev. 12:11).

Do not let the pain of wounding keep you from dispensing the healing power of your wounds. Your story deserves to be told and heard by others. You must tell others about how you were wounded, but you must have the right perspective about the people who wounded you. You play a major role in your story, but not the only role.

Know Their Role

If you want to have strength like Jesus, you must have a story like his. The story of Jesus Christ, as written in the four

Gospels, focuses most of our attention on the conflict of the cross. The Gospels do celebrate Jesus's successes, but they concentrate on his cross. As a matter of fact, during Jesus's trial, we do not hear of any celebratory advocates standing up for him. All we know about is his adversaries.

Jesus's adversaries were not consequential but instrumental characters in his story. The same can be said of your adversaries and the adversaries of biblical heroes. Think about it. You cannot fully appreciate Joseph's story without his brother's betrayal. You cannot appreciate David's story without Goliath and Saul. You cannot appreciate Israel's story without Egypt, Babylon, or Persia.

In each of these stories, the heroes not only went through trouble, but they grew through the trouble. God wants the same for you. He wants you to grow through your trouble. Unfortunately, much of the trouble you will grow through will come at the hands of your adversaries. Your adversaries will treat you bitterly, but it can make you better.

By the end of many of the heroes' stories in Scripture, we find them reflecting back on their adversity and adversaries positively. Joseph said to his brothers, "ye thought evil against me; but God meant it unto good" (Gen. 50:20). The psalmist said, "It is good for me that I have been afflicted" (Ps. 119:71). You too can have that same perspective and see your adversaries as advantages. Let's look at a few archetypical adversaries that God uses to form Christ in you and often indicate you are in the midst of some advantageous adversity.

The Sifted One

Everyone responds to pain, struggle, and conflict differently. Your response to your cross will differ from the response of those carrying a cross with you. In the same way that Jesus responded to his cross differently than the malefactors crucified next to him, so will you respond differently and uniquely from others who carry a cross before you. Interestingly, though, the response to your cross is not limited to firsthand experiences. Everyone who has an eye to see your struggle will respond differently as well.

Your holy hardship does not happen in a vacuum. The process is personal, but not private. There are close relationships that will be affected by this season of your life. Some of your closest allies and advocates may begin to distance themselves from you as you navigate this painful process.

I will never forget the time when my son was playing on his favorite Spider-Man fold-up chair. As my wife recalls the event, he was trying to do something superhero-like with the chair, and it flipped and hit him on the bridge of his nose. Immediately, his nose started bleeding. I was not at home at the time. I was in a minister's meeting at church when I got the phone call to come home and see about my son.

My wife thought he broke his nose, and the sight of his blood was overwhelming. She called me to handle the situation because she could not handle seeing her son in that kind of pain. Thankfully, his nose was not broken. However, the situation did provide a valuable lesson. My son's pain caused his mother to distance herself from her son because it hurt her to see him in pain. I drew closer, but his mom followed the situation from far off. Some of your close relationships may respond similarly to your trouble. Peter responded that way to Jesus's trial and cross.

Peter was one of Jesus's closest disciples. He was one of the three who saw Jesus transfigured and glorified with

Moses and Elijah. Peter was also the one disciple to whom the Father revealed the messianic identity of Jesus. Peter was the one who walked on water at the behest of Jesus's one-word command. Peter was also the one disciple who had a family member healed by Jesus's power.

In the last chapter, we learned that Peter was also an insider. He was one of the three disciples to whom Jesus disclosed the grief and agony of his soul. Jesus and Peter were close. However, in Luke 22:54, the text says, "Then took they him, and led him, and brought him into the high priest's house. And Peter followed afar off." Those same words, "Peter followed afar off," are repeated in the other synoptic Gospels as well (Matt. 26:58; Mark 14:54). Jesus's cross, like yours, causes people who may have once followed you closely to follow you from far away.

Do not be surprised if your pain and suffering causes people close to you to distance themselves from you. They may have said to you that they would be with you through thick and thin. They may have confessed their loyalty and commitment to stay with you for better or worse. They may have even stood up to other adversarial people in your life like Peter did with the temple servant, cutting off his ear. I would encourage you, however, to guard your heart, because those same people may distance themselves from you during your struggle and eventually act as if they do not know you.

Peter denied knowing Jesus three times. Denying a person really means you act as if you do not know a person. In a way, they do not know you. Peter was used to Jesus getting out of a jam quickly and smoothly. He was accustomed to Jesus walking in great power and being virtually untouchable. He was not used to a vulnerable Jesus. Your friends and family may not be used to you being vulnerable for a prolonged period either.

Examining Peter's behaviors in the Garden and at the high priest's house suggests a polarity that resembles the symptoms of grief. Peter violently cut off a man's ear, and less than a few hours later, he was in denial. Anger and denial are two stages of grief. Peter's response to Jesus's suffering was really a manifestation of grief. Peter was grieving the loss of his friend and master. Many of your friends will grieve during your process too.

Their grief should not surprise you. People who have strong feelings for you will take your pain the hardest. You should expect people who have yet to be inducted into the fellowship of Jesus's suffering to grieve your induction into it. Close relationships becoming a bit more distant for a season should not surprise you. It did not surprise Jesus.

Jesus not only predicted his arrest, suffering, crucifixion, death, and resurrection; he also predicted Peter's denial. Jesus predicted it and prepared Peter for it. Jesus knew that his suffering would create an opportune time for Satan to sift Peter.

Sifting is a process that separates what is useful from what is not. Jesus's passion provided an opportunity for Peter to go through his own process to become more useful in the future. Jesus took the initiative to warn Peter of his upcoming sifting and pray for Peter so the sifting would bring out the best in him; and Jesus, after his resurrection, reconciled with Peter after the sifting was complete.

There are some close relations in your life who will distance themselves from you for a season. Do not cut those people off. They may very well be enduring a sifting process to make them more useful in your life after your suffering is over. Do for them what Jesus did for Peter. Warn them, pray for them, and reconcile with them once your holy hardship is over.

Do not allow the way they grieve to create irreconcilable grievances between the two of you. Sifted people are integral to your future after the struggle is over. There will be some, however, who will never give you the opportunity to reconcile!

The Betrayer

The cross you bear comes with experiencing the pain of betrayal. Betrayal is a pain that cannot be experienced by the suspicious. You can only feel betrayal if you have loved and trusted the person betraying you. You cannot protect yourself from Judas. As Jesus did in the Garden of Gethsemane, you must embrace Judas. You cannot fulfill your mission without Judas. Judas did not usurp authority, and he ushers you into new levels of authority.

There are a lot of people out there who misrepresent Judas. They claim that some people are Judases when those people are probably Peters. Jesus knew the difference between Judas and Peter, and so should you.

The difference between these two archetypes rests in the difference of their breach of relationship with Jesus. Peter denied Jesus. He acted like he did not know Jesus. Peter denied Jesus to protect himself. He was trying to keep himself out of harm's way.

Judas, on the other hand, was not trying to protect himself. He was trying to promote himself. Judas was not acting like he did not know Jesus. His arrangement with the temple authorities hinged on the fact that he intimately knew him. Judas was not trying to stay out of harm's way, but rather, he put Jesus in harm's way.

A study of the episodes that identify the behaviors of these two disciples would show that Peter, throughout his tenure of discipleship, was incessant about keeping Jesus out of harm's way. He got rebuked for it twice: once, after Jesus's first prediction of his death, and then he was rebuked for cutting off the ear of a temple servant in the Garden of Gethsemane.

Judas, however, was an opportunist. Judas was vocal about how the woman with the alabaster box should have used such a precious gift. He was concerned about how he could leverage his relationship with Jesus for personal gain, even if it meant moonlighting with Jesus's enemies.

Peter was rebuked with the words, "Get thee behind me, Satan" (Matt. 16:23), and he was told that Satan sought to sift him as wheat. Peter was sifted by the devil. Judas was entered by the devil. The devil found in Judas a kindred spirit, the spirit of an opportunist. Your Judas is not like Peter.

Do not mistake denial or abandonment as betrayal, because Judas Iscariot was not the only Judas among the disciples. Luke records the name of a Judas the son of James (Luke 6:16) as one of the twelve. Judas the son of James abandoned Jesus after his arrest, just like the other ten disciples. Judas the son of James was not the same as Judas Iscariot, the betrayer of Jesus.

Here are a few more differences between Judas and Peter to help shape a Christlike perspective of your betrayer. Peter, after denying Jesus, wept bitterly. He grieved his loss. Judas hung himself after betraying Jesus. He grieved his gains.

Peter was eventually forgiven by Christ. Judas, however, could not forgive himself.

All these differences are important, but there is one major difference that identifies the heinous nature of Judas's betrayal and sets him apart from the deniers and abandoners. According to Scripture, the temple authorities and conspirators needed Judas to identify Jesus so they could arrest him. They needed Judas to take them to the Lord. The conspirators did not know what Jesus looked like, and neither did they know where he would be located. Jesus's identity and location was hidden to them; it was confidential.

Jesus practiced what he preached. He preached on praying in private, and that is what he did. The Garden of Gethsemane was his private or secret place for prayer. It was a place where he could engage the Holy Father intimately without the pressures of the public. Only the disciples, his insulators, knew the Garden was his secret place. Only the disciples knew his pattern of prayer.

Judas left the upper room early on the night Jesus was betrayed. He was not in the room when they decided to go to the Mount of Olives. Without being present in the room, his relationship with Jesus gave him access to Jesus's patterns and behaviors. Judas was an asset to the conspirators because he knew sensitive information. He knew Jesus's secret place.

The location of Jesus's secret place was held in confidence by the disciples. Judas breached this confidence for personal gain. Your betrayer, without whom you cannot finish your God-given mission, is a person who knows your secrets and your secret place, and they will disclose them to your adversaries for their own personal gain. Your denier, by definition, acts like they do not know you. Your betrayer can only be so because they know you so well.

Your process, your cross-shaped adversity, includes a betrayer. You cannot protect yourself against betrayal. Your love for others and the trust you have for people opens you up to that possibility. The only way to protect yourself from betrayal is to be unloving and suspicious. In other words, you can only protect yourself from betrayal by being something other than Christlike.

Your Christlikeness will provide someone close to you an opportunity to be an opportunist. Unfortunately, like Judas, you may never have the opportunity to reconcile. You cannot save your Judas from themselves. No matter how much you may want to reconcile, you may not get the chance, because it is hard for someone who cannot forgive themself to accept being forgiven by others.

You may be surprised by who your betrayer turns out to be, but you ought not be surprised that you have been betrayed. Loving and trusting people open themselves up for the pain of betrayal. I encourage you to do to your Judas what Jesus did to his: embrace him.

Your betrayer is a necessity to your mission and maturity into Christlikeness. He tests the limits of your love. He prepares you for power. Jesus was betrayed without becoming bitter. Jesus was villainized and victimized without becoming vindictive or vengeful. How he handled his betrayer showed that he could handle great power. The way you handle your betrayer will show you, God, and others that you can handle great power because you can handle great pain. Embrace your Judas.

The Conspirators

The crucifixion of Jesus of Nazareth was filled with agony. The etymology of the word *excruciating* has at its root the word *crucifixion*. The pain was not just biological, but also mental and emotional. As we have seen already, Jesus's suffering included a denial, betrayal, and abandonment of his closest allies. His adversaries were more accessible than his allies. Your holy hardship will reveal the hearts of many of your friends.

Despite knowing about Peter's denial and Judas's betrayal, I would imagine the emotional toll Jesus experienced was not any less real or poignant. Regardless of your foreknowledge, denial will still hurt. No matter how much advance notice you have about one of your close allies disclosing sensitive information to people who want to cause you harm, when it happens, it will still be painful. No matter how much you know about an upcoming surgery, the pain you experience during the surgery may be masked by an anesthetic, but your recovery will still be painful. Your adrenaline during your adversity may mask the pain of your emotional trauma, but when it runs out, and it will, the pain will still be there.

Most of the emotional pain caused by your allies can be classified as hurt. You probably will not be able to pinpoint one specific emotion to describe the pain. You will more than likely just feel hurt. They did not touch you, hit you, or cause you to bleed, but they did hurt you.

Ironically, the people who caused Jesus physical pain did literally hurt Jesus. They imposed upon Jesus their will. Jesus was hurt by his allies emotionally. The pain caused by his adversaries may not have been harmful to Jesus in the same way, but I can imagine it was frustrating mentally. I say that because of all the people who should have known better than to conspire to have a man executed, it should have been the chief priest and elders of Israel.

Jesus's conspirators were not seditious murderers with a history of crime and violence. Judas handed Jesus over to a mob that should have been in prayer and fasting, preparing for the Passover. Instead of fulfilling their biblical responsibilities during a high and holy time of Israel's feast calendar, they conspired to kill a Nazarene.

Stories like Jesus's and yours scream the age-old question, *Why do bad things happen to good people?* During your time of testing and trouble, that question will intensify significantly. Your trials, tribulations, pain, and frustration are not necessarily a result of your wrongdoing. You may be innocent of wrongdoing. You may be persecuted for doing right at the hands of people who supposedly are the standard-bearers in your culture for what is right. One of the most frustrating things about holy hardship and cross-shaped adversity is that bad things happen to good people at the hands of other "good" people.

Why do bad things happen to good people at the hands of other good people? Pilate, whom we will deal with in the next section, seems to offer some insight to ascertain the answer to that question. When the chief priest and elders brought Jesus to Pilate, he reluctantly heard their case because "he knew that for envy they had delivered him" (Matt. 27:18). Bad things happen to good people at the hands of other good people because of envy!

People who believe their "goodness" is a result of their works and not the work of God's grace are prone to envy. Envy is different from jealousy. As Bishop Noel Jones distinguished it in a sermon, jealousy is a fire for one's own, but envy is a fire for what another owns. Jesus was popular, charismatic, powerful, and morally excellent. Jesus was what the chief priests aspired to be but knew they were not. They were not healing the sick, raising the dead, feeding the hungry, or giving sight to the blind. Their power was limited to regulation and intimidation. They could not do what Jesus could, and they envied him.

Those who conspired against Jesus were members of a religious aristocracy. They were well educated and wealthy. They had cultural influence and status. Despite all of their advantages, influence, and affluence, they were envious of Jesus. Their envy became so visceral that it led to a conspiracy to crucify the Lord.

I want to pause here and ask you a question: Do you live, work, or worship with such excellence that it breeds envy in people who have more influence and affluence than you do? Here is a word to the wise: excellence begets envy, and envy begets conspiracy.

The Bible says that Daniel had an excellent spirit. Daniel was also the victim of a conspiracy that led to him to be thrown into a lion's den. David was an excellent warrior. David was a victim of a conspiracy at the hands of Saul. Joseph was favored but was also the victim of a conspiracy that landed him in a pit and enslaved. Moses was excellent, and his sister and brother conspired against him, as is told in the book of Numbers. The pattern is clear: excellence begets envy, and envy begets conspiracy. The only way to protect yourself from envy is to be average!

In each of the above cases, the envious parties were not followers, but peers or superiors. Your conspirers will be like the chief priest and elders. They will be morally astute, affluent, and influential. They may be pillars of the community and people you look up to. They will leverage that affluence and influence to carefully craft a conspiracy to assassinate your character and reputation. The good news is that they only have one bullet. The bad news is that they will not miss.

The narrative of Jesus's passion is not just an accurate account of history; it is a literary work of art. The writers of each Gospel form within the narrative of the Gospels an almost epic story of a heroic figure named Jesus of Nazareth. Jesus was a man in history. He is also a character in a story. The death of Jesus is literarily the death of a character in a story. If we interpret his death figuratively, we can conclude that his conspirators wanted to assassinate a character in the story. The agenda of the conspirators was character assassination.

Your conspirators have that same agenda. However, it is an agenda that they cannot execute alone. The good news is that even though they may have the will to assassinate your character, they do not have the power to do it. The bad news is that they are savvy enough to leverage their influence and turn you over to someone who has the power to execute their agenda, even if that person does not have the will to do it.

A Politician and a People Pleaser
Advantageous adversity is about understanding authentic power. Yes, it is immediately painful, but it is also ultimately profitable. God is setting the stage to enlighten you to the truth about power. No other cast of characters in Jesus's passion facilitated that enlightenment like this last group.

The politician and the people pleaser are adept professors of power.

Nestled in the passion narrative is the irony of power. Jesus was the Son of God and possessed the power to call twelve legions of angels (Matt. 26:53). He was a king whose kingdom was not of this world. However, as a monarch of a kingdom, he was tried without due process of the law, detained, and physically abused at the hands of people with less "power."

We can gather from Jesus's words in Matthew 28 and his temptation in Matthew 4 that, at the time of his crucifixion, he walked in heavenly power. His own words declared, after his resurrection, "All power is given unto me in heaven and in earth" (Matt. 28:18). The devil tried to offer Jesus earthly power without a cross, and Jesus refused.

Jesus had spiritual power, which is ultimately more powerful than any earthly power. He submitted to suffering at the hands of earthly power. The pain he experienced was not by virtue of being overwhelmed or overtaken by a power greater than his; it was the result of his submission to a cup in the Garden of Gethsemane (Luke 22:42).

There was not a point in the narrative of Jesus's passion when he did not have more power than others. His submission to the cross would not allow him to express the overt might of his spiritual authority. During the passion, Jesus's power was revealed in how much he could take, not how much he could deal out.

As you navigate the nuances of these nuisances, never forget that at no time do these archetypes have more spiritual authority than you. Your process may be painful, but that does not mean you are not powerful. The authenticity of your strength and power is revealed in how much of a "licking" you take, and you keep ticking. If you take the devil's best shot and still recover, then you, my friend, have the most power. Look at how much had to be done to crucify Jesus.

For Jesus to be put to death, it required a conspiracy among those with religious power to team up with a betrayer in Judas, a politician in Herod, a people pleaser in Pilate, and a popular criminal in Barabbas. Jesus's passion required the most influential people in Jerusalem to team up with the corrupt powers of Rome and immorally execute him. It took a lot of power to assassinate Jesus, and that was with him allowing it to happen.

Your pain is teaching you about your powers. I am not writing these words to create paranoia, but to give you perspective. Your pain is giving you privileged information about how powerful you are. No one person can be your undoing. Like Jesus, it is going to take a team. If you feel like there is a team of forces or people ganging up on you to facilitate your demise, you may be amid some advantageous adversity.

As I said in the previous section, the conspirators have the will to assassinate your character, but they do not have the power to do it. They have the "want to" but not the weaponry. Their agenda cannot be executed without making alliances. They can harm you, but they cannot assassinate your character. For that reason, they hand you over to someone with power to do so. In Jesus's case, it was Pilate.

The chief priest and the temple elite brought Jesus to Pilate after trying him in their own court. They had already beaten and mocked Jesus. They had already decided that he should die. They could have stoned Jesus, but they did not. Their agenda was to humiliate and shame him through crucifixion.

Pilate, upon trying Jesus, found no fault in him, knowing that the temple elite brought Jesus to him because they envied him. Pilate had no interest in facilitating the execution of the chief priest's agenda. Pilate operated as a judge in this case. Judges are supposed to be neutral. Neutral power, you will discover, is the most dangerous type of power.

An automobile in neutral can go in any direction if pushed hard enough. Pilate's initial reaction did not expose his true feelings about the situation; he just had not been pushed hard enough. Pilate, as he told Jesus, had the power to crucify, but he initially was not interested in doing so. Pilate exploited a loophole through which he could escape. He claimed that Jesus's fate was in the hands of Herod because Jesus was from Galilee, the region under Herod's jurisdiction. It just so happened that Herod was in Jerusalem that evening.

Herod, according to Scripture, was dying to meet Jesus of Nazareth. Further investigation would reveal that his desire, like that of his predecessors, was not genuine. The line of Herods had already sought to kill Jesus as an infant and killed Jesus's forerunner and cousin, John. The Herods had proven to be a murderous bunch. The Herod at the time of Jesus's trial was no different. Just as his relatives before him hid their true agenda for the Messiah, he did so now. Herod was the consummate politician.

Your induction into the fellowship of Jesus's suffering may facilitate an encounter with politicians who are, for our purposes, people under the active influence of the political spirit. Politicians are alliance makers. They build relationships to fulfill their agendas. The agendas of people under the influence of the political spirit are always hidden. The hidden agenda of a politician is usually cloaked with affirmation and adulation.

They will say they are really on your side, but they are not. Politicians believe there is only one side: theirs.

Politicians, unlike conspirators, do not throw rocks and hide their hands. Instead, they make alliances so they do not have to throw rocks at all. Herod wanted Jesus dead, but he did not want to be the one who executed him. Herod, being the quintessential politician that he was, sent Jesus to someone else so that he was not unpopular with his Galilean constituency.

According to Scripture, Herod formed another alliance that day, an alliance with someone who, up until that point, was an enemy: Pilate. One of the clear signs that you are being introduced to holy hardship is when you witness enemies become friends because of your demise. Luke 23:12 says, "And the same day Pilate and Herod were made friends together: for before they were at enmity between themselves." Your pain will make friends out of former enemies.

The death of Jesus of Nazareth would meet the political interest of King Herod. Politicians, however, want their interest fulfilled in a way that does not upset the people or cause protests. Jesus's popularity among Galileans would cause protest among Herod's constituency. Herod sent Jesus back to Pilate in hopes that Pilate would do what was in Herod's best interest. He wanted the rock thrown, but he did not want it to come from his hand.

Jesus's popularity was the reason why the religious conspirators arrested him and tried him under the cover of darkness. Ironically, it was in the dark that their agendas came to light. In order to execute their agenda, they knew they had to do so when Jesus's popularity would not protect him. The conspirators were in the minority, and they leveraged their influence and affluence to come across as the majority to Herod the politician and Pilate the people pleaser.

· When they returned to Pilate, they had no other options left but to continue to push a seemingly neutral person over the edge to crucify Jesus. By this time, the minority looked more like a mob, one with enough volume and vigor to achieve their agenda by pressuring Pilate. They could not convince Pilate of Jesus's guilt, but they could pressure him to put Jesus to death.

The conspirators and Herod knew that Pilate's interest was peace. Pilate did not want any riots among the rambunctious Jews during the Passover. There was always a heightened alert for insurrection during the Feast of Passover. Under imperial pressure, Pilate was disposed toward maintaining the Pax Romana. The mob of conspirators only had to intimate that they were ready to riot, and Pilate would fold.

Pilate didn't not crucify Jesus to please himself. He made it clear that he found no guilt in Jesus and that he did not want to crucify him. Pilate crucified Jesus to please the people in front of him. Pilate was a people pleaser. It was his will to do the will of the people. Instead of doing what was right, Pilate did what was popular.

Your season of privileged pain will introduce you to leaders who lack the courage to do what is right. They do not fear God. They fear the people. The common thread to this trio of the conspirators, politicians, and people pleasers is the fear of man! They fear the mob more than they fear the Messiah. They are moved by the will of the people, by the court of public opinion, or by the results of polling.

Your personal excellence and moral righteousness will cause you to look at these leaders with frustration. You will find it hard to believe that people with such great influence are so spineless and afraid. It makes no difference whether they got their influence or position by appointment or by vote; many politicians and people pleasers suffer from the same malady: the fear of man.

Proverbs says, "The fear of the LORD is the beginning of wisdom" (Prov. 9:10). The inverse of this statement would also be true: the fear of men is the beginning of foolishness. Pilate forfeited his judgment and wise counsel because he feared men. He could not make a wise decision. He could only make a decision of political expediency. His final decision was to let the people decide. He foolishly thought that this group of religious leaders would not choose a murderous insurrectionist over a peaceful and innocent Galilean. He thought he rigged the ballot and escaped the quagmire that he passively found himself in. Boy, was he wrong.

The People's Choice

Pilate, lacking the political will to crucify Jesus, set up a run-off election. He chose the most heinous and polarizing candidate he could find. His choice was Barabbas, who was in custody and scheduled to be crucified. Jesus's charge was proclaiming to be a king and Son of God. Barabbas was convicted of murder and insurrection.

The vote was an overwhelming landslide for Barabbas. Ironically, the name Barabbas is a compound word, meaning *son of the father*. The choice was between the authentic Son of the Father and a counterfeit son of the father. The mob, to Pilate's chagrin, chose the counterfeit. This is a choice you will see made as you enter and go through holy hardship.

The emotional peril of cross-bearing involves the disappointment of being authentically and genuinely anointed but not being the primary choice of the people you were called to serve. You are God's choice, but you will not always be the people's choice. You will wrestle with rejection during your trouble. You will scour your mind to find reasons for your rejection, and you will come up empty. What will deepen your feelings of disappointment is the fact that the people you are anointed to help chose a counterfeit over you. You worked hard to maintain your integrity and authenticity, but when it came down to it, you were still unpopular, and they gave the counterfeit something that should have been passed to you.

Let me be clear, Barabbas did not deserve to be released. He was not chosen because the people loved him. He was chosen because the mob hated Jesus. That is the catch of convenient popularity. The people's choice was popular because of their hatred for another, not for their love. You do not want to be the people's choice. You want to be God's choice.

As God's choice, you must learn how to navigate the nuances presented to you by a denier, a betrayer, conspirators, politicians, people pleasers, and the people's choice. You must learn to embrace your role in the narrative. Though they treat you like a villain, remember that you are the hero. You can help them, even though they do not want you to serve them.

The mob chose a counterfeit that day, but the cross proved that Jesus was the real deal. Counterfeits are chosen to avoid their cross. The authentic are chosen to bear theirs. When you wonder why they did not choose you, remember what you have been chosen for, and it will tell you who you were chosen by. You have been chosen for a cross, which means you have been chosen by God!

YOUR CROSS AND
ITS TESTIMONY

Every cross is tried in the court of heaven and the court of public opinion. Hardship will put your identity and character on trial. You must be wise about when and where to provide your testimony during your cross-shaped adversity.

Jesus provided little to no testimony during his trial in the temple court or with Pilate. In the more than thirty thousand words Jesus spoke in the synoptic Gospels alone, less than 150 of them were spoken during his time in the court of the high priest and the Roman procurator.

The writers of the Gospels made it a priority to point out Jesus's lack of words during his trial. Matthew says that when Jesus was asked to respond to the witnesses against him, "Jesus held his peace" (Matt. 26:63). Even John marveled at Jesus's restraint and tells us that during Jesus's trial with Pilate, "Jesus gave him no answer" (John 19:9).

In contrast to the silence of the Lamb during his trial, we find a speaking Jesus on the cross. While Jesus was on the cross, he quoted Scripture from Psalm 22. He also uttered the words "I thirst" in order to fulfill Scripture (John 19:28). Jesus's words from the cross seem to suggest that Jesus thought the cross, not the court, was the best platform from which to give his testimony.

The words of the centurion at the cross would suggest that the cross, not the court, was indeed the best place for Jesus to testify. It was after seeing a dying but vocal Jesus on the cross that the centurion was convinced about the veracity of Jesus's claim and identity. When the centurion saw Jesus cry out and give up the ghost, he said, "Truly this man was the Son of God" (Mark 15:39). The best place for you to offer your testimony is not in the court of public opinion but on a public cross.

Nothing to Prove

Walter Brueggemann, in his book *Truth Speaks to Power*, examines the narrative of Jesus before Pilate. In this exchange, Jesus and the procurator talked about truth. John says that Pilate, upon hearing Jesus talk about truth, asked, "What is truth?" (John 18:38). Brueggemann points out the irony of the defendant knowing the truth and the judge being ignorant of it. Jesus knew the truth, and that is the revelation he held onto during his passion. What was the truth? The truth is that Jesus is the Messiah, the Son of the living God!

Jesus had a firm grasp on the truth about his identity and purpose. Truth about who you are and your relationship to

God is the one thing you must hold on to during a season of suffering. No matter how hard it gets, no matter how painful, no matter how unbearable, remember who you are and who you are to God.

Jesus stood accused of saying that he was the Messiah, the king of the Jews, the Son of God. The chief priest did not believe that Jesus was the Son of God. During Jesus's trial with the Sanhedrin, he was asked directly if he was the Son of God: "Art thou the Christ, the Son of the Blessed?" (Mark 14:61).

Mark's Gospel was written in such a way that Jesus's true identity was concealed throughout the narrative. For example, in contrast to the baptismal affirmation of the Father in Matthew, where a voice from heaven was heard by the crowd saying, "This is my beloved Son, in whom I am well pleased" (Matt. 3:17), Mark's affirmation seems to suggest only Jesus heard the Father say, "Thou art my beloved Son, in whom I am well pleased" (Mark 1:11). Additionally, Jesus was the only one to see the heavens open and the Spirit descend upon him (Mark 1:10). The only characters in the Markan narrative who knew Jesus's true identity were demons (Mark 5:7), the blind (Mark 10:47), and Peter (Mark 8:29). It is not until Jesus's trial that Mark's Gospel starts the ascension to literary climax where Jesus himself reveals his true identity. How would Jesus, who in other parts of the narrative quieted demons and told those he healed not to tell anyone about it, respond to the chief priest's questions? Mark 14:62 records Jesus's long awaited answer in the first clause: "And Jesus said, I am."

At this point in Mark's Gospel and others, the mob got hostile and asked Jesus to prove it. They wanted Jesus to provide evidence to support his claim. They blindfolded him, hit him, and asked him to prophesy who it was that struck him, since he was the Christ. Jesus offered no evidence. Jesus did not try to defend himself.

In the face of violent accusation, Jesus did not react, resist, or retaliate, because of his resolve. He knew the truth. It did not matter who believed him. Their belief or lack thereof did not change the truth. Jesus's resolve about the truth of his identity empowered him to resist the temptation to defend himself and prove himself.

There is a discipline within the church that is geared toward offering a defense of our faith. Defending the faith in our tradition is called apologetics. The term derives from ancient Greek legal jargon. In the Greek legal system, when a defendant stood accused, they were expected to offer a defense or an apology. In this sense, Jesus offered no apology for being the Son of God. He was unapologetic about his identity. You should have the same revelation and resolve about who you are! During your hardship and adversity, you should be unapologetically you.

As you go through your time of testing and suffering, there will be a constant temptation to prove that you are a child of God. Resist it. Your identity is not contingent on circumstance. You must believe that you are God's beloved even when there is no circumstantial evidence that proves it.

Jesus, in Luke's Gospel, answered the question of the chief priest by saying, "If I tell you, ye will not believe: And if I also ask you, ye will not answer me, nor let me go" (Luke 22:67–68). Jesus understood that the only people who ask for proof are those who will not be convinced by it. Do not try to prove yourself to people who would not believe the evidence if they saw it! Unapologetically embrace your identity without feeling obligated to prove yourself. Your antagonist, your situation, and your circumstance are vehement because some people are uneasy by your unapologetic resolve to be yourself!

Being yourself requires no defense when you know who you are. Jesus's resolve to be himself was the main reason why he offered no defense. He exercised his right to remain silent. "As a sheep before her shearers is dumb, so he openeth not his mouth" (Isa. 53:7). "Who, when he was reviled, reviled not again; when he suffered, he threatened not" (1 Pet. 2:23). Isaiah prophesied about Jesus's resolve. Peter witnessed the resolve firsthand. Jesus's refusal to prove himself was the proof that he was the Christ. Your refusal to retaliate and respond is the proof that you are the child of God you say you are.

As the intensity of your adversity increases, make a commitment to save your breath. Do not waste your time, words, or breath trying to prove yourself to people. Do not respond to people or circumstances that will not be changed by disclosing the truth. Hold your peace. Do not argue. Do not apologize. Do not leverage your talents and gifts as weapons. Remain silent. Save your breath, because you are going to need it!

Breathtaking Pain

Growing up the son of a Baptist pastor, I heard my fair share of sermons. I heard my dad practicing his sermons as he got ready for church. I traveled with my dad as he preached revivals every week during the summers of my childhood. I heard a lot of preaching. Out of all the sermons I have heard, one has stuck with me. I cannot remember the title, but I do remember the content. My father used to preach a sermon about the physical brutality of Jesus's suffering.

Hearing the graphic details of Jesus's flogging and cruci-fixion imbued the scene upon my conscience and soul and brought new meaning to the words of an old hymn: "what pain, what labor, to secure my soul from endless death."[1] My dad's sermon taught me about the process of Roman flog-ging. He preached about how the Romans used a flagellum to cause the most pain to flogging victims. A flagellum was a whip made by the Romans. They would take a "cat o'nine tails" and place into it glass, iron balls, bones, and other flesh-piercing objects. The iron balls would soften the skin, and the other objects would tear the skin.

In my father's sermon, he talked about how the victim would usually pass out because of the pain. He then shared that the soldiers would wake the victim up by placing alcohol and other tonics in the wounds. They would use the flagellum and flog the victim across the back, shoulders, thighs, and buttocks. Many victims never made it to the cross because of the blood loss and pain from the flogging.

In the military and police forces, individuals with the most noncommissioned rank wear stripes on their arms to signify their authority. Newcomers into these forces who desire to ascend the ranks of authority must earn their stripes. Stripes are connected to authority. Isaiah says of the suffering servant, "with his stripes we are healed" (Isa. 53:5). The healing authority of our savior came at the expensive cost of the stripes caused by a Roman flagellum. Your ability to provide comfort and healing to others will come at the cost of you earning your stripes. The painful process you are enduring is building your spiritual authority and power.

By the time the cross was placed on Jesus's shoulders, he had already lost a significant amount of blood and sleep. He would have been extremely exhausted and fatigued when they placed the seventy-five- to one-hundred-pound patibulum across his battered shoulders to walk to Golgotha. A patibulum was the crossbeam that people condemned to die by crucifixion would carry to the post upon which they would be impaled. Jesus would have done so as long as he could by carrying it up a hill on bruised shoulders.

The Messiah, according to Isaiah 9, was said to have the government upon his shoulders. The condition of those shoulders was revealed in Jesus's crucifixion. Jesus carried the weight of an entire species, and he did so with bruised, bleeding, and battered shoulders. His ability to carry his cross revealed his strength being made perfect in his weakness. God will also prove to do the same thing as you carry your cross.

The pinnacle of pain for our Lord came at the top of a hill called Golgotha. The scriptures at this point give no details about the crucifixion. One Gospel simply says, "there they crucified him" (Luke 23:33). My dad, however, did his homework and gave detail to the process and anatomic intricacies of the crucifixion.

Jesus's body was already racked with pain, his shoulders worn out from carrying a cross on shoulders that endured the trauma of a flagellum. On Golgotha, he was no longer in control of his own body; he was under the control of his executioners. They would have laid him on the patibulum and nailed him to the cross with spikes that measured over nine inches long. As my dad explained it, the nails would not have gone into the palm of his hands but into his wrist. The bones in the hands were not strong enough to support the crucified body's weight. The executioners drove the nails through the wrist so the victim would not fall off the cross.

The nails in the wrist would shoot fire-like pain through the victim's forearms, biceps, and shoulders. They would also cause the hands of the crucified to form a claw. After impaling the victim to the cross, they would, by rope and pulley, lift the victim up so they could place him on the vertical post placed there for crucifixions. Once lifted upon the post, the executioners would bend the legs of the condemned, cross his feet, and nail his feet to the vertical post.

The outstretched arms and bent legs of the victim created a constriction of oxygen. The crucifixion made it difficult for its victims to breathe. For Jesus to breathe, he would have had to push down on his nailed feet and stand on the cross so that he could inhale. Straightening his legs would rub his battered back, lacerated thighs, and bruised shoulders against the splintered wood of the cross. The pain would have been excruciating.

The Romans perfected crucifixion as a tool of torture. Jesus's blood loss from his beatings was not the cause of his death. His beatings, shock, and lack of sleep weakened him so that he could not physically do the constant up and down on the cross to keep oxygen going through his body. The cross was death by asphyxiation. The cross tried to take Jesus's breath away.

We join Jesus in a fellowship of his suffering when we endure breathtaking pain because of our identity in him. You will not be impaled to a wooden cross like Jesus was. You may, however, endure your own metaphorical flogging by which you earn your stripes. You may also feel the weight of the world on your shoulders. And you will endure some breathtaking pain.

Breathtaking pain is the kind of pain that makes it hard to praise God or pray to him. Psalm 150:6 says, "Let every thing that hath breath praise the LORD." It is easier to praise God when you have financial breathing room. It is much easier to praise the Lord when you are not undergoing a process that is taking your breath away. It takes wind to praise God. It takes breath to speak.

Jesus decided to offer no defense during his trial. He remained silent. However, once he was hoisted upon the cross at Golgotha, he started speaking again. Jesus said more from the cross, when it was most difficult to breathe, than he did during this trial. Our Lord did not waste his breath defending himself against his adversaries. He saved his breath for his cross!

It Hurts Me to Say This

Among the last words of Jesus from the cross were "It is finished" (John 19:30). The Gospel of John discloses this phrase of Jesus during the crucifixion. John does not position the cross as a victimization of Jesus, but rather as a glorification of the Son of God. John gives us a glimpse into Jesus's perspective of the cross. Jesus saw the cross as part of his work, not part of his worries.

The mindset of Christ in this regard is alluded to when Jesus said, "Now is my soul troubled; and what shall I say? Father, save me from this hour: but for this cause came I unto this hour. Father, glorify thy name" (John 12:27–28). Jesus connected his cross to a glorious cause. Christ did not view his suffering as a random act of injustice. He was indeed murdered, but he was also martyred. Jesus suffered for a reason, a cause. His suffering had meaning because it was connected to his ministry! His cross was a part of his life's work. Jesus was on the cross working until, with one of his dying breaths, he said, "It is finished."

Jesus provided services from the cross until that very statement of finitude. The work of our Lord was one of ministry, miracles, and teaching. The gospel shows us that Jesus did more with his voice than he did with his hands. It was with his voice that he calmed a raging sea. Jesus's words, and his words only, healed the centurion servant. Jesus's words healed ten lepers. It was the voice of the Lord that raised Lazarus from the dead. Jesus wrought more miracles with his voice than he did by the laying on of his hands. Even from a cross, our Lord continued to use his voice to teach and work miracles. On the cross, Jesus was literally working through his pain.

When I say Jesus was working through his pain, I mean that in two senses. Jesus's words from the cross were a part of his mission, ministry, and work. He was teaching while in pain. He was providing ministry through his pain. In another sense, Jesus had to work or fight through his pain.

For Jesus to speak, he had to get enough air into his lungs. As we discussed in the previous section, the cross was an instrument of torture to suffocate its victims. Jesus had to lift his battered body up to get enough air into his lungs for him to speak. Imagine the pain Jesus felt in his arms, back, legs, and feet every time he decided to open his mouth to speak. Imagine the agonizing pain of splintered wood scraping the open wounds on his back that were placed there after a full night of "earning his stripes." Consider the sharp pain in his forearms and shoulders from the nails in his wrist, jolting piercing pain through his arms as he braced himself to pull himself up on the suspended cross.

Jesus had to work through his pain to work through his pain. Each of the seven last words of Jesus were spoken with one hard-earned breath. Every breath was worked for, painfully. It hurt Jesus to say everything he said from the cross. The significance of his work was greater than the suffering of his work. Your life's work is too important and significant for you to remain silent while you suffer.

Your cross is connected to a glorious cause. The significance of your mission requires you to work through the pain to keep working through the pain. The cross will teach you about your most valuable work asset: your voice. The power of life and death is not in the hands of a Pilate; it is in your tongue, even while you are experiencing breathtaking pain.

Our Lord was suffering from a lot of things on that cross, but laryngitis was not one of them. You must teach through the pain, preach through the pain, lead through the pain, and nurture through the pain. You, my friend, must speak through the pain.

I want to offer you a truth you must grasp and understand while you work through the pain. There will come a time during your season of suffering when you cannot remain silent. You will have to speak, and to do so, you are going to have to lift yourself up to talk. There are some things you are going to have to say from your cross, and it is going to hurt you to say them.

It is going to hurt to tell the people who are causing you pain that you forgive them. It is going to hurt to talk to the Father in prayer. It is going to hurt to talk to people who are suffering because they are watching you suffer. It is going to hurt to help others who are in a similar place but for different reasons.

One of the most painful things I have had to do was preach to a congregation who, less than twenty-four hours prior, made a motion to vote to remove me as pastor. I did not have a hard time preaching to them when I found out that a petition to have a specially called church meeting was circulating during a funeral service at another local church. I did not have too much of a tough time delivering the Sunday sermon the week before the meeting was held, even though the meeting was never announced in church. The petitioning party kindly left flyers on the windshields of the cars in the parking lot during Sunday service. Of course, my car and the cars of many of my advocates did not receive flyers. Many of those actions and steps were cause for concern but did not make preaching difficult. The Sunday morning after the meeting, however, was the hardest sermon I ever preached.

The moderator of the meeting, from reports I received, explicitly told the congregation that the meeting was not about removing me as pastor. He said it was to express concerns about the state of the church. For the next three or so hours, witnesses were called to disclose sensitive and confidential information about me to the congregation. Many of the witnesses against me were people I considered to be advocates who turned out to be adversarial or neutral at best. Additionally, a two-page document was drafted by the petitioning group listing all of their grievances against me, and unfortunately, they expressed complaints about my wife. I had not done anything illegal, immoral, or unethical. Obviously, I had done some things that were unpopular.

After three hours of hostile testimony, someone made the motion to vote to remove me as pastor. Ironically, the moderator, who said the meeting was not about voting me out, kindly picked up the voting ballots he brought to the meeting that he hid under the table.

What made preaching that next day so difficult was the fact that the vote was never taken. Another motion was made to place the issue into arbitration. My ministerial career would hang in the balance for another two months. The church was in an uproar and still hostile. I learned the results of the meeting from a concerned advocate at the church. I was not welcome at the meeting to defend myself. None of the church's deacons informed me of the decision or how the meeting unfolded.

I did not rest that Saturday. I was anxious, vulnerable, and scared. I did not know what I was going to be walking into the next day. For the first time in my ministry, I had to preach about the cross from a cross. That Sunday, I did not just need a message; I needed a model. What was I supposed to say to a crowd of people filled with hecklers, adversaries, and silent advocates? How was I supposed to preach something holy in the midst of so many who were hostile? Thank God Jesus had to do it long before I did.

Holy versus Hostile

Jesus's seven last words provide for us a pattern for how to speak from our crosses. It will not be easy to speak the way he spoke. As I mentioned in the earlier section, it hurt Jesus to say everything he said from the cross. It hurt him physically. It will hurt you emotionally and mentally. The emotional and mental toll stems from the reality that you will be attempting to do something holy in a hostile environment.

The crowd at Golgotha was not the easiest crowd to speak to. Many of them were hostile. The cross was not the easiest platform from which to testify. The cross hurts. Cross-shaped adversity will demand that you do something holy in a hostile environment.

You will have to speak to a crowd like the one Jesus had before him that day. They wanted to hear what Jesus had to say, but they did not want to listen to what he had to say. The crowd contained conspirators, hecklers, executioners, and supporters. Of Jesus's close circle, only John the beloved disciple was there with Jesus's mother. It is clear from the biblical record of Jesus's passion that most of the crowd were not sympathizers or supporters of his. In fact, you never hear any of his supporters say one word to Jesus while he was impaled to the tree. The overwhelming stress of your situation may cause people who support you to be present but remain silent.

On the contrary, the conspirators and hecklers spoke to Jesus more than any other group. They questioned his identity. They tested him several times. They made it painfully and publicly obvious their feelings about Jesus of Nazareth. You must make it clear how you feel about "them." Your words carry your witness. The test will challenge you to speak something holy that can be heard over the hostility.

Cross-Shaped Prayers

We often preach the seven last sayings of Jesus during Holy Week. I think we may want to preach and learn from what Jesus did not say from the cross. Jesus only used the word *them* once in his seven last sayings. When he used that word, it was in regard to a prayer he lifted from the cross to his Father. The prayer was an address to his Father for "them." He said, "Father, forgive them; for they know not what they do" (Luke 23:34).

"Them" and "they" were the loudest and most antagonistic bunch at the cross. They derided him, railed him, challenged him, and tested him with their words. Jesus, however, did not go back and forth with his hecklers. He only referenced "them" once. It was his first word from the cross, and it was a word of forgiveness. After asking the Father to forgive them, he never spoke about or to that group in the crowd again.

Technically, Jesus never spoke to them. He spoke to the Father about them in a prayer. Jesus prayed for the people who were preying on him. Jesus did not just teach about praying for your enemies; he demonstrated it! The people who cause you pain during your hardship should not be the subject of your sermons, presentations, or emails; they should be the subject of your prayers. They will not listen to you speak to them about God, but God will listen if you speak to him about them. Jesus teaches us that no matter how loud our "haters" or "enemies" get, we should never talk to them directly. We should talk to him about them. Your testimony should be that when they preyed on you, you prayed for them.

Jesus asked that the Father not hold against them what they were doing against him. Whoever your "them" or "they" are in your life, make sure you pray for them. Pray for them like Jesus prayed for his enemies, from the discomfort of a public cross instead of the comfort of a private closet. Your cross is a great place from which to pray. The same holy act that got you through Gethsemane will get you through Golgotha.

Of the seven last sayings of Jesus, three were directed to his Father, one was directed to a penitent thief, one was directed to his mother and beloved disciple, another was directed to the Roman soldiers, and one was directed to the crowd in general. God the Father was the audience Jesus spoke to the most! Jesus talked to the Father about forgiveness and forsakenness, and with his last breath, he commended his Spirit to the Father.

Your testimony contains within it more than just preaching. It contains cross-shaped prayers, the kind of prayers you say while in pain and, more importantly, hurt you to exclaim them. There are going to be times in your suffering season when it is going to hurt to pray. You will not feel like praying. You will be too tired to pray, too wounded to pray, too frustrated to pray, too angry to pray. My advice is to pray anyway.

Your heavenly Father is the only one who can handle all your frustrations, anger, confusion, and anguish. Pray angry. Pray confused. Pray wounded. Pray frustrated. Just pray.

Public speaking coaches will tell you that people remember the first and last things you say during a keynote presentation. The first and last words Jesus said from the cross were prayers directed to his Father. The crowd would not just remember that Jesus suffered; they would remember how he suffered. Jesus's cross-shaped prayers did not reveal that he was a fraud but that he was authentically righteous and the Son of God. Jesus did not get out of hand when things got out of hand. He trusted the Father and put things in his hands. With the words "Father, forgive them; for they know not what they do" (Luke 23:34), he turned over to the Father those who turned him over to Pilate. With the words "Father, into thy hands I commend my spirit" (Luke 23:46),

Jesus put himself in the Father's hands. When things get out of hand, you should put your adversity, your adversaries, and yourself in the Father's hands. You do this through cross-shaped prayers.

Your Testimony and Those Who Listen

Jesus's cross-shaped prayers revealed that, during all his pain, he was acutely aware of the presence of God the Father. Your pain will not be more acute than his presence. Prayer reminds you and those in the crowd that you are not alone. The crowd may be against you, but God is still with you. The cross did not keep Jesus from being God with us, and it did not keep the Father from being God with him.

Even the passionate prayer asking, "My God, my God, why hast thou forsaken me?" (Mark 15:34) suggests an awareness of the presence of God. Jesus would not waste his breath speaking to someone who could not listen or was not there.

You are not alone in your suffering. Of course, the crowd is there, but God is there too. You may feel forsaken, but God is still there with you. He may not be present to intervene in your situation, but his is still present. It may feel like he has left you, but he still loves you. You are not alone.

As a matter of fact, there are other people going through the same thing you are going through. Jesus was not crucified by himself. He was impaled to an instrument of torture between two malefactors, two thieves. Those two thieves were enduring similar physical pain, but for different reasons. They also talked to Jesus from their crosses. Jesus, however, only responded to one of them.

The two malefactors, as the Bible calls them, requested two different things from Jesus. Only one request received an answer from the Lord. Jesus indeed heard both requests, but only one of them engendered a response. The exchange between these three men proves that God hears all but does not answer all.

One of the thief's prayers was not so much a request but a dare. The Gospel of Luke says, "And one of the malefactors which were hanged railed on him, saying, If thou be Christ, save thyself and us" (Luke 23:39). The term "railed on" means to speak bitterly. While the cross was bringing the best out of Jesus, it was bringing bitterness out of one malefactor. The words of this bitter request are strikingly like the words Satan used to tempt Jesus: *if* you are Christ. The bitter thief wanted off of his cross and desired that Jesus use his power to make it a reality.

As the second thief shares with us, both thieves deserved to be on their crosses. They were sentenced to death and were guilty of their charges. The second thief responded to the first so Jesus didn't have to, saying, "Dost not thou fear God, seeing thou art in the same condemnation? And we indeed justly; for we receive the due reward of our deeds: but this man hath done nothing amiss" (Luke 23:40–41). In other words, he was saying that we may not be on our crosses for the same reason, but we are all in this thing together.

Everyone does not respond to suffering the same way. The guilty and the innocent suffer together and respond differently. Some guilty sufferers become bitter through their pain, and others become sober. I believe the second thief was being sobered by his suffering. He did not want to come down off his cross. His request of Jesus revealed that he saw in Jesus what most others in the crowd could not see. He saw what the other thief was too bitter to see.

The sober thief declared Jesus as king and Son of God long before the Roman centurion on the scene did. His request proves it to be so. This malefactor said, "Lord, remember me when thou comest into thy kingdom" (Luke 23:42). He believed Jesus was a king. He also believed that both he and Jesus had a future after the cross. He requested to be a part of Jesus's future. Jesus responded with a royal declaration from a place of pain. "Verily I say unto thee, Today shalt thou be with me in paradise" (Luke 23:43).

Jesus did not invite the sober malefactor into his pain, but he invited him into his paradise. You should do the same for others as Jesus did for the sober thief. Do not let the cross make you bitter. Allow your cross to reveal the best in you. During your time of trial, test, and suffering, you will run into other people who are going through a similar trial and deserve to be going through it. Not everyone on a cross is innocent. However, the cross is doing for them what your cross is doing for you: bringing you closer to Jesus.

The sober thief did not request to come down because he knew he was right where he was supposed to be, and he was honored to be closer to the Christ because of it. He did not ask to come down because he knew that if Jesus was on the cross with him, staying on the cross was the best place for him. The sober thief's cross did for him what your cross is doing for you: revealing your closeness to Christ. The second thief considered his cross a privilege because of the proximity it granted him. He used his request to move from pain to paradise.

As you speak from your cross, make sure you speak to the sober thieves. Speak to others who are going through the same thing you are but for different reasons. There are some people who suffer and do not want to escape the consequences of their deeds. They do not suffer innocently, but soberly. For many of these guilty sufferers, their pain and suffering is drawing them closer to Jesus. Your cross and theirs may create an opportunity for you to invite them into a relationship with Christ.

You can win souls through your suffering. Who are you inviting into paradise while you are in pain? Do not allow the cross to make you self-righteous and lose your compassion for sinful sufferers. The way you handle your cross may open someone's heart to Jesus. Our faith does not exempt us from suffering; it empowers and equips us to handle it.

The words Jesus spoke to the second thief prove that the cross does not have to take your compassion. There are people enduring what you are enduring, but they are not believers. They do not need to be condemned; they already are, and they need compassion. Can you give to them the kind of compassion the crowd refuses to give to you?

Are you suffering in such a way that nonbelievers can see a future paradise through your suffering? Do you have the compassion, empathy, and power to invite others into a paradise while you are in pain?

Do not invite people into your pain, as most people are already there; invite them into paradise! The only way for you to offer that kind of invitation is to believe that you have a future that is better than what you are going through right now. In fact, your pain is paving the road to paradise. There is a bright future ahead of you! I hope you believe it.

Suffer with the future in mind. Jesus endured the cross and despised the shame because of the joy that was set before him. You have a future after the cross! If Jesus rewarded a thief's faith with fellowship in paradise, how much more will he reward your faith while you are inducted into the fellowship of his suffering?

Remember, do not invite others into your pain; invite them into your paradise. An invitation into paradise from a cross requires that you have faith in your future! This is not the end! Testimony from a cross is believable because the cross has not robbed you of faith for the future! There are suffering people watching your suffering, and they believe that there is a glorious future ahead of you. Invite them into that future with you! Jesus made room in the fellowship and his future for thieves, and we should too! There is room in the fellowship for the faithful and for thieves!

Your Unfinished Business

Not everyone witnessing your situation is enjoying what you are going through. There are people who still care about you. Painful seasons in our lives can bring with them a certain blindness to the fact that the entire world is not against us. You still have people in your corner who are invested in your success and cannot stand the sight of you suffering. They feel helpless because they know they cannot stop the pain or intervene. They understand that the situation you are in is not accidental, but providential. However, they do not enjoy seeing you go through so much agony and pain.

The people who care enough about you to be present while you are on a cross are like Mary and the beloved disciple. These two people came to the cross, but unlike the crowd, the soldiers, and one of the thieves, never opened their mouths to say a word. They were silent sympathizers.

You will discover, often to your dismay, that there are people on your side who care about you but are not in a place to express their feelings because of the pressures of all the haters and gainsayers in your life. They will not defend your character or reputation. They will not provide testimony or evidence to the conspirators, politicians, and people pleasers who are invested in your calamity. They may not be vocal, but they care.

Do not alienate your silent sympathizers. They care about you. It hurts them to watch what you are enduring. Many of them are silently angry, silently frustrated, and silently distraught. It is not the time for you to associate their silence with compliance. I said it before and I will say it again: they care about you. They are taking a risk to stay close to you during your time of hardship. They took a risk that some of your insiders, intercessors, and insulators would not take. Make sure to show them love, and reciprocate the care.

I hope I am making my point clear. If not, I will repeat my point. Hear me clearly: there are people witnessing your situation who care deeply about you! Their silence is not a sign of compliance. It is a sign of wisdom. Ask yourself, what could they say or do to make things better? Mary and John's presence at the cross was all the comfort they could give Jesus. You have some friends and family who cannot give you any money, advice, or strategies. They cannot offer you any solace, but they can offer you their silent presence.

If you have never faced extreme peril, take it from me: sometimes just knowing a person who cares about you is there is enough to keep you focused and fighting, especially if the person caring for you is someone you care for. When you are in a hospital, you have nurses who are present and paid to take care of you. Their presence is comforting and helpful, but it is not the same as the presence of someone you love being in the hospital room with you.

In the previous section, I shared that you should not let the cross rob you of your compassion for guilty people enduring similar circumstances. You also should not allow your circumstances to steal your compassion for innocent people who are not suffering like you are. When people show you that they care, make sure to reciprocate the gesture.

Mary and the beloved disciple cared for Jesus. More importantly, Jesus had a responsibility to care for them. These two people were not random bystanders; they were family and a follower. Jesus, like you, had to continue taking care of people while being crucified. The predicament and the pain did not abdicate the Lord from his responsibility as the oldest son of Mary and the teacher of John. Your adversity will not exempt you from continuing to care for your family, employees, congregants, or constituents.

Adversity does not happen while you are on vacation. It happens while you are on the clock. Your children will still need help with their homework. Your spouse will still need support and attention. Your job will still expect results, on time and on budget. Your circumstance requires that you execute your responsibilities while being executed yourself.

You cannot have any unfinished business during this season of your life. You cannot take a break from being responsible. You still must make sure the people you care about are taken care of. Jesus's words to Mary and John made sure that his mother would be taken care of after the cross. Mary, his mother, took care of him; now Jesus, her eldest son, was taking care of her. Both did so at a time of excruciating pain.

You may feel forsaken on your cross, but it does not give you the right to neglect your responsibility to those you care about. Pain can make you self-centered. It can make you focus on how you need to be taken care of. It can make you focus solely on your needs. Self-centeredness while suffering leads to bitterness, and you see where that got the bitter thief on the cross.

You must remember that your cross may take your comfort, but not your identity. You hold the highest office in the kingdom, a son of God. Sons of God have authority whether they are pristine or in pain. In the kingdom, authority only goes to those with responsibility. If you have responsibility, you have authority. Jesus could promise the thief paradise because he had authority. He could make arrangements to take care of his mother because he had responsibility.

You may be in pain, but the pain does not rob you of identity, authority, or responsibility. You still have the power and the responsibility to take care of business. Do not endure your season of suffering with unfinished business. You are still a father, mother, business owner, president, superintendent, or mayor. You are still a son, daughter, sister, brother, husband, or wife.

You may have to care for others while in need of care for yourself, but you take care of others anyway. You may wish that someone would care for you like you care for other people, but you care for other people anyway. You may alleviate their pain with no antidote or anesthesia for your own pain, but you alleviate their pain anyway.

You are more powerful than you think you are. Your cross is revealing the true source of your power. Jesus made sure to take care of his mother even with his hands tied. The true source of his power flowed from his identity, not his ability. Your identity as a son or daughter of God is the true source of your strength. The cross cannot rob you of your identity. You still have the power to take care of your responsibilities while you are suffering.

You do not have to allow the stress and strain of your situation to deplete you of your will to continue taking care of business. Your cross can strengthen you to finish your Father's business. I encourage you to execute your responsibilities, especially when others are trying to execute you! Leave nothing unfinished. Your role as a son or daughter of the Most High is too valuable to leave any unfinished business.

Unfinished business is not about exacting your revenge. It is about continuing to execute your responsibilities amid daunting circumstances and breathtaking pain. Revenge is beneath the dignity of the office you hold as a child of God. Jesus not only taught like a king; he suffered and died like one. He maintained the dignity of his identity and was responsibly obedient until the end. You have that same kind of strength in you. Your cross will help you find it.

Keep Your Head Up

The Gospel of Mark shares with us an episode in Jesus's passion that preceded his crucifixion. After scourging Jesus, the company of Roman soldiers "clothed him with purple, and platted a crown of thorns, and put it about his head" (Mark 15:17). Mark goes on to say, "And they smote him on the head with a reed, and did spit on him, and bowing their knees worshiped him. And when they had mocked him, they took off the purple from him, and put his own clothes on him, and led him out to crucify him" (Mark 15:19–20).

The Roman soldiers crowned the Lord with a crown of thorns and commenced to beat that crown into his brow with a reed. Scripture makes sure to tell us that Jesus's punishers and executioners took off the purple they gave him, which indicates that they did not take off the crown. Jesus had to suffer the pain of nails in his hands and feet; stripes on his back, shoulders, and legs; and thorns stabbing him in the most vascular part of his body: his head.

Of all the scars and physical trauma Jesus endured, the crown of thorns was most emblematic of the irony of the cross. A crown is a symbol of authority and power. Thorns in Scripture represent vulnerability and a curse.

God told Adam that the ground would yield to him "thorns also and thistles" because of his disobedience (Gen. 3:18). Jesus's parable of the sower spoke of the thorns that choke the word out of those who hear it. The apostle Paul spoke of a thorn being given unto him to buffet him. He called his thorn a "messenger of Satan" (2 Cor. 12:7). Thorns were not symbols of power, but of pain.

Jesus was crowned with what buffeted Paul, what choked the word out from others, and what Adam was cursed to yield to from the ground. He was the king of thorns.

Imagine the headache Jesus had while impaled to the tree. Imagine the blood that poured into his scalp, hair, eyes, and mouth from the thorns that were beaten into his brow. He would not have looked strong and powerful like most kings do. He would have looked weak and vulnerable.

Andy Crouch, in his book *Strong and Weak*, argues that true human flourishing can only be experienced at the intersection of authority and vulnerability.[2] Humans, he suggests, were created to have authority and vulnerability. The crown of thorns is a symbol of human flourishing. The crown represents authority; the thorns represent vulnerability.

Jesus's crown was custom-made. They platted it. Your crown of thorns will be customized for you as well. It may feel like you are only vulnerable, but the crown is a symbol of authority. You may be racked with pain, but you still have royal power. Jesus proved that he was vulnerable enough to suffer, but not at the cost of his authority to govern.

The chief priest and scribes conspired against Jesus to have him crucified so they could embarrass and shame him. They wanted him to die in the most undignified manner possible. Stoning Jesus would not be enough. Poisoning was not enough. They wanted Jesus publicly shamed and humiliated by suffering the most heinous execution known to man.

Jesus, however, did not give them the pleasure of recanting his claim to the thrones of heaven and earth. Jesus did not whine or complain about his pain. Jesus did not hold his head down in shame. Jesus maintained the dignity of his identity through all the pain until the very end!

John's Gospel tells us a minor but revelatory detail about how Jesus suffered on the cross. He tells us that Jesus, after giving up the ghost, "bowed his head" (John 19:30). John makes sure that we know that Jesus did not bow his head until after he said, "It is finished" (John 19:30).

John's minor detail about the position of Jesus's head after his last word suggests to us that Jesus spent the entirety of his time on the cross with his head up! He was able to balance the symbol of authority and vulnerability under severe circumstances. He endured the cross and despised the shame with his head held high.

He suffered, bled, and died like the king he claimed himself to be. He suffered with dignity! The cross did not rob him of the dignity of his royalty.

As you suffer your own cross, make sure to do so with your head up! I know it hurts, but keep your head up. I know you are misunderstood, but keep your head up. I understand you are frustrated and angry, but keep your head up. Do not let the pain of your process rob you of your dignity; rather, allow it to reveal your royal dignity.

You have no reason to hold your head down. You have no reason to be ashamed. Keep your head up, and eventually some of the same people who helped create your customized crown will verify that you are a daughter or son of God. Your success will not convince them, but how you suffer will. When it is time for you to testify from your cross, make sure you do it with your head up!

NOTES

[1] Charles Wesley, "Father, I Stretch My Hands to Thee," 1707.

[2] Andy Crouch, *Strong and Weak: Embracing a Life of Love, Risk, and True Flourishing* (Downers Grove: InterVarsity Press, 2016).

YOUR SURRENDER AND THE WAITING

Trouble does not last forever. Your cross-shaped adversity has a distinct timetable. Your suffering cannot and will not last forever. It may feel like it will never end, but that feeling is betraying the truth. Your process will expire. It will finish before you are finished.

Jesus's hardship ended with the words, "Father, into thy hands I commend my spirit: and having said thus, he gave up the ghost" (Luke 23:46). If Jesus's adversity did not last forever, neither will yours.

The scriptures provide a theme about the nature of holy hardship. It is pain for our profit. Here I use the word *profit* in the sense that the writer of Hebrews used it in Hebrews 12:10: "For they verily for a few days chastened us after their own pleasure; but he for our profit, that we might be partakers of his holiness." The text is making a distinction between human chastening and sovereign chastening. Humans chasten after their own pleasure, but God chastens for our profit. The crucifixion proves this point. The chief priest and other conspirators crucified Jesus for their pleasure, but God sovereignly allowed it for both our and Jesus's profit.

The nature of sovereign suffering is that the trauma eventually transforms into triumph. Psalms says, "Weeping may endure for a night, but joy cometh in the morning" (Ps. 30:5). The psalmist also said, "They that sow in tears shall reap in joy" (Ps. 126:5). Jesus said, "This sickness is not unto death, but for the glory of God" (John 11:4). Paul said, "For our light affliction, which is but for a moment, worketh for us a far more exceeding and eternal weight of glory" (2 Cor. 4:17). Holy hardship never ends in tragedy. It always ends in triumph.

Suffer with the Next in Mind

The truth that sovereign suffering never ends in tragedy is alluded to in Hebrews 12:2, which says that Jesus "who for the joy that was set before him endured the cross, despising the shame, and is set down at the right hand of the throne of God." Jesus endured the suffering because of the joy that was set before him! He endured the trauma because he knew about the eventual triumph.

Jesus's foreknowledge of his eventual triumph is alluded to in his passion predictions. Jesus's passion predictions were really about the resurrection, not the cross. There was not a moment of Jesus's suffering when he was not aware of the promise the Father made to him. Jesus knew that he would be raised again in three days.

A victim of crucifixion would normally take several days to die. In fact, if it took too long for the crucified to expire, the executioners would break his legs to accelerate death. Jesus gave up the ghost after several hours on the cross, not several days. The speed of Jesus's death seemed to come as a surprise to Pilate. In response, Pilate requested that a soldier make sure Jesus was dead. The soldier, instead of breaking Jesus's legs, pierced him in the side. The blood and water that ran out was proof that the spear pierced Jesus's heart and that he was dead.

Jesus prophesied that he would be in the earth for three days the same way Jonah was in the belly of the fish for three days. Jesus knew that he was not to be resurrected from a cross, but from a grave! Jesus knew there was more to his passion than just his public suffering. He suffered with the next in mind.

You will not endure the pain of sovereign suffering if you do not have the "next" in mind. You cannot make it through Good Friday unless you have Resurrection Sunday in mind. Pain can only be a privilege if it is connected to a promise. We endure it all for the joy that is set before us.

You Must Give Up

Your pain has an expiration date because your promise has a due date. Jesus knew that he would rise from the dead in three days. He knew his trouble would not and could not last longer than its appointed time. Jesus's appointment with destiny superseded his appointment with death. Your appointment with promise supersedes your agony and pain.

Jesus gave up the ghost at the hour when he did because he understood where he was supposed to be next. Jesus's promise required that he finish his work on the cross and give up! Your holy hardship will require you to do the same. Bearing your cross will eventually lead you to a point where you must give up.

I am not telling you to quit. I am not advocating that you give in. I am advocating that you give up. The last words of Jesus indicate a unique way in which he gave up the ghost. Before taking his last breath, he said, "Father, into thy hands I commend my spirit" (Luke 23:46). Jesus gave his Spirit to the One above him. He literally gave something up!

Jesus did not give in to his captors, conspirators, or critics. He did not quit. Jesus surrendered to the Father. He put things in his Father's hands.

In several of the passion predictions, Jesus told the twelve that he would be "delivered into the hands of sinful men" (Luke 24:7). Jesus was betrayed into the hands of men and suffered many things at their hands. However, after the work of the cross was done, he no longer had to remain in the custody of sinful men. Jesus's last words indicate that he was no longer in men's hands but in the Father's hands.

David believed that God's hands were better to be in than in the hands of one's enemies. After numbering the people against the will of God, David was given a choice of consequence for Israel. "And David said unto Gad, I am in a great strait: let us fall now into the hand of the LORD; for his mercies are great: and let me not fall into the hand of man" (2 Sam. 24:14). Even in a great strait because of his wrongdoing, David would rather suffer at the hands of God than at the hands of men. If it is better to be in God's hands than men's hands when you are a disobedient son, how much better is it to be in God's hands when you are being an obedient son?

During my adverse season, I had a conversation with my father. I was scared, frustrated, confused, and a host of other emotions. I wanted God to do something and turn the situation around. At the time, I did not know that sovereign suffering was God's way of letting you know you are chosen. I reached out to my dad, who is a pastor, for advice and counsel. After sharing with him the things I was going through, he got quiet on the phone. The silence was so thick that I had to ask if he was still there. His next words shook me to my core. He said, "Son, you're in his hands now, and those are the best hands you can be in."

At the point when my dad and I had this conversation, my situation was not over. Neither was Jesus's at the point when he commended his Spirit into the Father's hands. The process was not over, but the worst of it was. Surrendering into the Father's hands does not represent the end; it represents a shift. When you surrender to the Father, you are no longer at the mercy of men.

My father's words to me and Jesus's words from the cross provided comfort because, by them, I knew that I was no longer in "their" hands. If you have reached this point in the book, I want you to rejoice because there comes a point in your process when you are no longer at the mercy of men. You are no longer in their hands. You may not be fully restored, you may not be totally healed, but at least you are no longer in their hands.

Once Jesus gave up the ghost, there were still soldiers with weapons who were commanded to wound him. Jesus was pierced in the side after his death. There will be some who will attempt to wound you after you have surrendered.

However, because you have surrendered, their weapon will not prosper. For Jesus, the worst was over.

Posthumous Piercing

Jesus gave up the ghost, but some had not given up wounding him. John's gospel narrative suggests that Jesus, though deceased, was not out of reach of wounding. Of all the trauma Jesus endured, there was still one wound he would be given after his death.

According to John, the Jews did not want the two thieves or the remains of Jesus's body to hang on their crosses during the Sabbath day, so they compelled the soldiers to help expedite the execution. The common practice of that day was to break the legs of the crucified so they would no longer be able to raise themselves to get the necessary air to keep breathing.

"Then came the soldiers, and brake the legs of the first, and of the other which was crucified with him. But when they came to Jesus, and saw that he was dead already, they brake not his legs" (John 19:32–33).

Jesus, having surrendered to the Father and given up the ghost, was already dead and did not need for his legs to be broken. The executioner, however, was charged to make sure that the crucified was indeed dead. The soldiers' next move is helpful in understanding what our holy hardship looks like after we have metaphorically given up the ghost.

The soldier took a spear and pierced Jesus in the side. John makes special note that "blood and water" came out forthwith (John 19:34). The spear would have done more than pierce the skin; it was intended to pierce the heart. The soldier's actions would have either verified that the crucified was dead or hastened the crucified's death.

If Jesus were not dead at the time the soldier's spear pierced his side, only blood would have evacuated the wound. A beating heart would have still been pumping blood only. The heart of a deceased person contains a mixture of blood and a watery-like plasma due to the sedimentation of the blood in the heart of the deceased.

The Roman executioners were trained on how to provide proof of death from a victim of crucifixion. Piercing the side to pierce the heart yielded undeniable results. Jesus was in fact dead at the time of the piercing.

The unnamed solider had to take these measures because six hours of crucifixion was not the normal length for someone to die on the cross. Jesus's unique suffering and surrender accelerated the process.

You should consider this as you contemplate your own surrender. Surrender accelerates your growth into Christlikeness so that you are safe from harm even when others wound you. God may allow the weapon to form, but when you give up the ghost, that weapon will not prosper.

The posthumous piercing of Jesus had a purpose and was undertaken to do a couple of things. First, the soldier did it to make sure Jesus was dead. It guaranteed that he was dead. Second, but more importantly for us, it was done to fulfill Scripture.

God has a way of granting power and permission to those out to harm you so that by their hands you can fulfill prophecy. Your advocates may seem helpless in assisting you to achieve your mission; however, God can orchestrate situations to allow your adversaries to help you fulfill destiny. After you surrender, unknowing enemies will help you reach your goals.

John tells us that the scriptures spoke of Jesus propheti-
cally so that "A bone of him shall not be broken" (John 19:36).
Another scripture that was fulfilled exclaims, "they shall look
upon me whom they have pierced" (Zech. 12:10; John 19:37).
One act after Jesus's surrender fulfilled these prophecies, the
Word was still working after Jesus's surrender and death.

These two texts should give you hope and peace, for they
promise that if you suffer with him, you may be pierced but
you will not be broken. The pain may pierce you, but it is not
intended to break you. As a matter of fact, the final blow of
your situation will come at a time when it cannot ultimately
harm you.

Posthumous piercing is perhaps the devil's way of deter-
mining if you have really surrendered! The enemy knows how
surrendered disciples respond to his wiles and weaponry.
Once you claim to be surrendered by giving up the ghost,
you can expect a test of that declaration. The only way to
pass that test is to "play dead."

Playing Dead

Before I continue, a word must be said about the metaphorical nature of suffering as Christ suffered. Jesus was literally
and historically crucified. He experienced the pain and
suffering of the most excruciating form of torture and execution of his time. Many of the twelve apostles of the Lamb
would suffer the same fate of crucifixion. Other martyrs were
eaten by beasts in coliseums, burned alive, beheaded, and
underwent many other heinous forms of persecution. In our
modern age, there are still physical persecutions happening
among the faithful around the globe. They will truly have
their reward.

Advantageous adversity does not require that believers literally be impaled on a cross or experience physical persecution that leads to martyrdom. We experience real suffering and metaphorical crucifixion. The apostle Paul, who experienced physical persecution, wrote in the book of Galatians that he was "crucified with Christ" (Gal. 2:20). He wrote this while he was yet alive. He also spoke of being dead to sin and other metaphorical references to death. His references to crucifixion and the death of believers did not involve nailing them to trees until they took their last breath. We are encouraged to pick up crosses and die to self metaphorically.

What you may be going through or have gone through is causing you real pain, anguish, and suffering. Your hardship is a metaphorical crucifixion and requires a metaphorical death. You must surrender as a disciple of Christ unto a metaphorical death. Metaphorical death has real implications on your behavior in the real world. The metaphorical death requires you to "play dead." Playing dead does not change how you breathe; it changes how you behave.

You already know that I am the son of a pastor. What you do not know is that my dad also owns and operates a funeral home. I have seen my fair share of the physical remains of a formally living human being. Growing up, my sisters and I would often "play dead" because of the many times we would go to the funeral home to visit my father at work. We would imitate the postures and mannerisms (or the lack thereof) of the deceased as they lay "asleep" in the casket.

To win our morbid game of playing dead, we would have to endure creative attempts by our siblings to get us to come out of character. We would be poked, tickled, screamed at, called by name, and a host of other creative tactics to test the level of our "deadness." Even as children, we had a sense of the difference between the living and the dead when it comes to behavior.

The posthumous piercing you endure is the enemy's way of getting you to act out of character after you have surrendered. You maintained your dignity and character through the gauntlet of trials during your holy hardship. Like Jesus, you have learned to remain silent and unapologetically be yourself. You have learned how to leverage your voice, saying things that hurt you to say while you are publicly humiliated. You have kept your head up during the entire trial and maintained your character as a disciple. Now that you have given up the ghost and put yourself into God's hands through surrender, you no longer have an obligation to respond to the wiles of the devil or anyone he uses as a weapon. You have come a long way. Now is not the time to come out of character.

The piercing of Jesus's side was significant because it corroborated his declaration about laying down his life, saying, "No man taketh it from me, but I lay it down of myself" (John 10:18). If Jesus were to have had a death certificate, the cause of death would not be suffocation, but surrender. The spear of the Roman soldier would not get the glory for killing Jesus. The spear did not kill him; surrender did! The cross was an instrument, not a cause.

God wants the glory from your surrender, and you must maintain that surrender even when circumstances and situations arise to test your surrender and get you to act out of character.

One of the foremost characteristics of a deceased person is the lack of response to outside stimuli. No matter what you do to the body, it never responds. The dead do not resist. They do not put up a fight.

It is imperative that you maintain your surrender by not resisting or responding to the metaphorical spears of others. You must resist resisting others. You must fight the urge to put up a fight.

You will be tempted to tweet a response. You will be tempted to post a response on Facebook. You will be tested and tried by false interpretations of your story. You will be agitated and aggravated by the deluge of questions about how you are doing. You will be tested by the frustration of receiving messages and phone calls about your well-being from people you know are only calling so they can gossip about you.

You will want to respond. My advice is to resist resisting against others. Do not respond. Put the phone down. Log out of Facebook. Delete the Instagram app. Close your Twitter account. Stay dead! There will be a more appropriate season for you to respond, but for now, maintain your surrendered posture and play dead. The dead do not respond. The dead offer no resistance.

I am so grateful for the coaching and advice I was given during my holy hardship. I will never forget the conversation I had with my pastor during this season. When I wanted to respond and resist the onslaught of accusations and continued agitations from others in my environment, my pastor would remind me that the greatest fighters learn to use their opponent's momentum and attack to their advantage. He called it leadership judo.

I am not a martial arts expert, and neither is my pastor. However, his advice was extremely helpful. He told me that in judo, you use your opponent's attack against them by not resisting. Instead of offering a counterattack against your enemy, you redirect the energy of their attack back toward them by not resisting the attack. He said that instead of wasting your energy, leverage theirs.

He went on to say that in a battle, the crowd wants to cheer for the protagonist. However, when both parties are attacking each other, it is hard to discern who to cheer for because both parties are antagonistic. When you offer no resistance, your opponent looks more like the antagonist, leaving you to look like a protagonist, thereby winning over the crowd.

Jesus offered this principle of leadership judo by instructing his followers to "turn to him the other also" (Matt. 5:39) when they have been smitten on the right cheek. Turning the other cheek is difficult because it requires you to offer no resistance to injury. There will be a situation, a person, a rumor, or an act that hurts you, and you must maintain your irresponsive disposition, regardless of the pain. Retaliation is not allowed in the fellowship of his suffering. A surrendered disciple looks forward to vindication, not vengeance.

The only way for you to maintain your surrendered disposition is understanding that you have already won the victory. Prior to Jesus giving up the ghost, he said, "It is finished." He completed his mission. He finished his work. He won his fight with death.

Victorious fighters are brought to the center of the ring and announced with the referee standing close by to physically acknowledge the fighter's victory. Once the fighter's name is called and his victory announced, the referee takes him by the hand and raises his arm. Most fighters will raise both hands to signify victory.

Raising both hands is a sign of victory in a fight, but it is also a sign of surrender! Surrender is a sign of victory! You do not have to fight anymore because you have already won. You do not have to respond to the agitation, pain, or provocative proclamations of your antagonist because you are already victorious. Posthumous piercing is the equivalent of the loser in a fight hitting the champion after they have been declared the winner. A champion gets nothing out of striking an opponent after they have secured victory; neither should you.

Resisting resistance is difficult because, unlike the literal dead, you can feel the pain. You must feel the pain and offer no resistance anyway.

In addition to offering no resistance, you must also do the hard work of depending on others. Dead persons cannot move on their own. They depend on others to get them around. Giving up the ghost requires that you trust God and trust others to help move you to the place where you can be restored and raised.

Jesus told his disciples that he would be in the earth for three days, just as Jonah was in the belly of the fish for three days. How was a dead Jesus going to get to a grave? Jesus had nowhere to lay his head while alive, so it is most likely that he had no place to lay his head in death. Roman authorities usually left the dead remains of the executed on the cross for days. For Jesus to make it to the prognosticated location, someone else would have had to get him there.

Analogies have their limitations, and we run into one here. Jesus was literally dead and could not move on his own. You and I are playing dead; we can still move, or better yet, we can still "make moves." You are more likely to make moves independently of others after a betrayal, denial, and conspiracy against you.

Jesus's closest allies abandoned him. The eleven, except for John, did not show up to the cross to witness Jesus's execution. The fulfillment of Jesus's Jonah prophecy would not come to pass because of the aid of Jesus's closest allies. After giving up the ghost, Jesus had to depend on help from unlikely people to get him to a place of fulfilled promise.

Help from Unlikely Places

As the deceased remains of Jesus of Nazareth hung on the cross, so did the fulfillment of the prophecy he declared in Matthew. When asked for a sign of his power and authority, Jesus replied to the interrogating parties of the Pharisees and the scribes: "An evil and adulterous generation seeketh after a sign; and there shall no sign be given to it, but the sign of the prophet Jonas: For as Jonas was three days and three nights in the whale's belly; so shall the Son of man be three days and three nights in the heart of the earth" (Matt. 12:39–40).

Jesus was prognosticating his resurrection from the dead and from a particular place. Jesus was prophesying his resurrection from a grave. For that prophecy to be fulfilled, it would take God to resurrect Jesus, but it would also require some human agents to take him down from the cross and put him in a tomb. Jesus was not going to get to the grave on his own or by the power of God!

Surrendering to God or giving up the ghost does not mean that God is going to do everything for you. Surrender is not a mere resignation of effort on your part to rely solely on God for everything. Surrender is about a holy resolve that the plan of God for your life will be fulfilled. More importantly, it is a resolve that God's plan will be fulfilled his way. Your surrender in this stage of your adversity gives you permission to experience who God is going to use to help you fulfill your God-given destiny and become a better person. God rarely uses who you would expect.

As I mentioned earlier, Jesus's most trusted and closest allies were tucked away in a safe place hidden for fear of the Jews. The eleven remaining disciples, save John, did not come to Golgotha to witness the execution of their master. No help was going to come from those closest to Jesus. Do not be alarmed if some of the people you were closest with and spent the most time with are farthest from you and have no time for you in your time of need. Do not hold it against them. They have distanced themselves from you because of their fear, not their true feelings. God has already provided other people in your life to help you get to a place of restoration and vindication. You must stay surrendered without strategizing what your next move should be to bring you closer to the power that comes from advantageous adversity.

The same God you trusted enough to submit yourself into the hands of the sinister men who put you on the cross is the same God you must trust to put you into the hands of helpful men who will take you off your cross. Your cross is constructed to restore relationship between God and others, as well as you and others. Cross-shaped adversity is redemptive and restorative. Your holy hardship should bring you closer to God and also closer to other people.

Orthodox Christian theology professes that Jesus was fully human and fully divine. The two natures of Christ exist in a unique relationship in which one nature does not diminish the other. Our faith in Jesus Christ is not just a faith in God. The two natures of Christ would suggest that our faith in him is simultaneously faith in God and faith in a human being. You cannot believe the God in Christ without believing the man in Christ.

God is going to use this process of your Christlike pain to restore your faith in him and in humans. You must trust God to restore you, but you must also trust who he chooses to use to get you to a place of restoration. Your surrender requires you to overcome your suspicion.

Playing dead, giving up the ghost, or surrendering requires that you depend on others after so many people have harmed you. Mature disciples of Jesus know how to trust God and appropriately trust people. You may feel abandoned, betrayed, forsaken, and alone, but there are some people in the crowd who are silent and secret admirers of yours. Your suffering may have drawn them out of the cave to a new place of boldness. There are people who may not have been close to you then that are waiting for an opportunity to help you get to a better place.

Luke gives us some clue as to who is available to help Jesus get from the cross to the grave. "And all his acquaintance, and the women that followed him from Galilee, stood afar off, beholding these things" (Luke 23:49). Notice the word *acquaintance*. The people who beheld the unfolding trauma of the cross were not Jesus's closest disciples, but his acquaintances.

Luke goes on to disclose the name of a man who sat on the counsel that conspired to kill Jesus but did not consent to Jesus's death. This man was a good and just man, and as Luke describes, he waited for the kingdom of God. Joseph of Arimathea was not one of the eleven, but he took it upon himself to go to Pilate and ask for the body of Jesus. The Gospel of Mark uses another term that intensifies Joseph's appeal to Pilate. Mark says that Joseph "craved the body of Jesus" (Mark 15:43).

While the eleven distanced themselves from Jesus, Joseph craved the body of Christ. Can you sense the intense affection Joseph of Arimathea had for Jesus? He craved to take care of a body that had ceased to breathe. He craved to be a caretaker for someone who had dedicated his life to taking care of others. No matter how hard things get in your life, God reserves a few acquaintances who crave to take care of you. God would not allow you to be in the hands of crucifiers if he did not provide a path for you to be placed in the hands of craving caretakers.

Joseph of Arimathea was not alone in his desire to take care of the body of Christ. John's Gospel identifies another affluent man in Jerusalem who initially came to Jesus by night, but after Jesus's death, aided in caring for Jesus's body. The curious secret admirer of Jesus named Nicodemus aided Joseph in the burial of our Lord. Nicodemus offered helping hands and other resources to take care of the body of Christ after he had given up the ghost.

The gospel narratives about both these men imply that they secretly admired Jesus. Neither of them is said to offer defense or witness on Jesus's behalf during his trial. They were not advocates of Jesus during his trial, but advocates after his death.

As adversity unfolds in your life, you will experience the frustration of secret admirers who have the power to be advocates but instead remain silent. You cannot allow that frustration to keep you from accepting their aid after you have finally given up the ghost. Their silence was sovereign, just like your suffering. Their advocacy and aid were providentially withheld until the right time.

Consider the exile of the Jews in Persia. There were probably numerous calamities that befell God's people while under Persian rule. However, Esther the queen only provided aid and advocacy for one situation. She was prompted by a poignant question: "Who knoweth whether thou art come to the kingdom for such a time as this?" (Esther 4:14). Joseph and Nicodemus shifted from being secret admirers to being public advocates at the right time for the kingdom.

There are some people in your life who have been resourced to take care of you. They may be secret admirers. They may behold things unfold in your life from a distance. They may even be among the same people who conspire to harm you. Regardless of their relationship with you now, you must have a place in your heart for the Josephs and Nicodemuses of your life. The fulfillment of your promise depends on how you learn to depend on people like them.

The Bible offers some details about Joseph of Arimathea's appeal to Pilate. It also offers some detail about the amount and components of the mixture Nicodemus brought as they prepared Jesus's body for the sepulcher. The Gospel writers offered no details about how Joseph and Nicodemus took the body of Jesus down from the cross.

Without biblical details, we are left to imagine this process, rely on the stories of others, or deduce some things about the process by common sense. In any case, thinking about this process does provide some insight to how you must think and behave in your surrendered state to the care of others.

The first observation about how Jesus was taken down from the cross involves the height of the body. We do know from the Gospel of John that crucifixion required a lifting up. Jesus was lifted above the height of most men and women. When he cried out "I thirst" (John 19:28), it required a sponge to be placed on a reed and given to him. Piercing Jesus in the side required a spear, not a sword. All this would suggest that taking Jesus down would require an instrument to prop up the caretakers so they could take the spikes out of his hands.

The common-sense tool of choice would be a ladder. Joseph, Nicodemus, or whoever they designated would have had to climb a ladder to get the nails out of Jesus's clinched hands. Climbing a ladder would mean they would have to step up.

You must trust that other people in your life are going to step up to aid you in recovery. After you have suffered awhile, you are in no shape to recover on your own. The vehemence of your suffering may have caused some of the people closest to you to step back, but rest assured, sovereign suffering will providentially provide the right people in your life to step up.

There are some people in your life who have secretly admired you from a distance who now have an opportunity to minister to you and aid in your recovery. Do not allow the pain of previous relationships keep you from enjoying the benefits of new relationships. Give other people the space and chance to step up.

You will only delay your restoration by waiting on your Peter, James, and John. Your caretakers may not be insiders, intercessors, or insulators, but they are no less valuable.

I want to encourage you to surrender fully to this process, because your restoration will not come at the hands of the people you think or want. You must trust the people God trusts to take care of you!

You cannot move forward and finish the process of becoming like Christ with fear and suspicion. Just as Jesus's surrender was tested with the piercing from the soldier, your surrender will be tested during the process of separation from the tool of your torture.

A ladder is one tool needed to take a person off a cross. Jesus's caretakers would also have needed another tool: a hammer. The same tool used to impale Jesus to the cross would have been used to help take him down.

Imagine the force needed to nail a person to a piece of wood so that they would hang there for days. Think about the sound of the hammer and nails as they are muffled by the screams and moans of the victim of crucifixion. It may have sounded like spikes going into railroad tracks. Now consider the horror of Jesus's acquaintances as Joseph or Nicodemus picked up the hammer to beat the nails back out of Jesus's hands.

An instrument of torture can be used as an instrument of release, depending upon whose hands it is in. Unfortunately for us, we have literally surrendered, but we are metaphorically playing dead. We are still alive to see our caretaker approach us with the same instrument that hurt us. Therefore, you must overcome suspicion, because our God-sent caretakers may have to use some of the same tools that our traumatizers used in order to help us move on.

You must fully surrender, because people will look like they are going to do you harm, but they are really sent to help you. You must let them help you. It may sound the same, it may even look the same, but there is one difference. The difference between a centurion and a caretaker is their heart and hands.

In the right hands, a hammer can be used to build. In the wrong hands, it can be used to kill. You must trust the hands God has put you in.

During my holy hardship, I had to submit to the hands of a licensed counselor. I was in counseling for over a year. It took that long to separate me from the torture of my trauma. Even after being physically distant from the people and place of my pain, I was still close to how it felt emotionally and mentally.

My counselor was not and is not a close friend. My counselor was not and is not someone I ministered to or worked with in the past. Without any significant connection in our past, my counselor was just the person I needed to help me move on from the cross.

Not every counseling session was consoling and empathetic. Many of them were challenging and full of constructive critique. If I had not surrendered to the process, I could have easily thought that my counselor was criticizing me like others had. I could have easily been suspicious of my counselor telling my story to others.

Coming off the cross is just as much a process as picking one up. As a matter of fact, Jesus was crucified by experts but was taken down by people with a heart but with no real expertise in cross removal. In other words, coming down from the cross probably took longer than being lifted onto one. You and I must give our caretakers space and grace to be who God called them to be to us.

They are called to help us move on. They are called to help us get to the next place on our journey. They are called to take us away from our place of trauma and lay us into a place of rest, restoration, and resurrection. Your caretakers may not be who you think they should be, but trust me, they are exactly who you need them to be.

Saturday Seasons

God places the right people in your life during times of intense pressure and pain to help you move forward. You do not have to stay in a place of trauma or despair. You may not have the strength to get over the pain on your own, but God will make sure that there are people in your life to help take you to a place of rest and restoration.

God provides these key people in your life because he has a timeline for your recovery. The bad news is that you cannot rush your recovery. The good news is that the devil cannot stop your recovery. It is imperative, however, that you are patient.

Jesus's passion narrative gives us details about the length of his stay on the cross and the length of his stay in the grave. If you calculate the time from Jesus's prayer in the Garden to the time he gave up the ghost, it would be much shorter than three days. Jesus's Garden prayers, betrayal, trial, denial, and crucifixion did not last twenty-four hours. His stay in the grave, however, was much longer than that. He had less than a day to die and more than two days to be raised.

Most surgeries require less time to complete than recovery from surgery. The recovery time is not calculated by the patient. The doctors determine the length of time needed to fully recover from surgery or injury.

Your recovery from injury, conspiracy, pain, or trauma is determined by God. You cannot determine how long before you are fully recovered; neither can your traumatizers, sympathizers, or conspirators. Your time is in God's hands.

Jesus was not able to make the declared recovery time any shorter. After all, he had given up the ghost. He could take no action to accelerate his recovery. He would be in the place where his caretakers laid him for three days.

In the Christian tradition in which I was raised, we believe that Jesus was crucified one Friday, and that he was buried and got up from the grave early Sunday morning with all power in his hand. Growing up in my home church, I heard a lot of preaching about Friday and Sunday, but not so much about Saturday. It was almost like Saturday did not count. Saturday seemed to be an obstacle to Sunday. I'd never heard anyone preach or mention the term "Holy Saturday."

Have you ever wondered what was going on in the grave the Saturday before Resurrection Sunday? Scripture provides little detail about the occurrences and happenings of Holy Saturday. We can, however, deduce the relative sentiments of those outside of the grave given how they responded to the news of Jesus's resurrection.

The Romans, the chief priest, the Sanhedrin, and the disciples had a similar response to the news of the empty tomb. They were all surprised.

The Romans and the Jews took special measures to ensure that the tomb of Jesus would not be tampered with. Pilate and the chief priest settled on specific measures to discourage any conspiracy of Jesus being raised from the dead. They assigned a watch to Jesus's tomb, and they placed a seal on the tomb.

Contrary to how I always thought about the seal, the seal was more of an insignia than anything else. The stone was not placed on the tomb from fear of the body of Christ being stolen; it was customarily placed to limit the stench of a rotting corpse. The seal was an insignia placed on the tomb as a sign that the Roman government would exact severe consequences on anyone who broke the seal.

Jesus's close followers were surprised by the open tomb when they came to the sepulcher early on the first day of the week. Like the chief priest and Pilate, they were surprised by the empty tomb.

This means that no one expected Jesus to come back to life. His enemies and his followers expected him to be exactly where they laid him. They did not expect any changes to occur from Friday to Saturday or from Saturday to Sunday. On Saturday, from the outside of the tomb, it would have looked like nothing had changed, was changing, or would change, ever!

Saturday, from the outside of the tomb, there would have been no signs of life or hope of a resurrection. This is the essence of a Saturday season.

Saturday seasons may last a day, they may last a quarter, and they can last for a year or more. They are characterized by an absence of hope for new life, restoration, or change among people who observe your situation.

As you recover from your traumatic and painful experience, you will also have to learn how to navigate relationships with people who believe that you will never come back from what you have been through. If they were asked on Saturday, Jesus's friends, followers, and foes would have all agreed that Jesus was never coming back. You will also have family, friends, and foes who are convinced that your recovery is impossible. They will mistake your surrender to God as resignation or quitting.

You must maintain your discipline and commitment to a surrendered heart and posture. You are in recovery and cannot afford to waste energy trying to prove to people that you have more ahead of you than behind you. You must not assimilate the perspective of the people outside of the tomb. From outside the tomb, it looks like nothing is changing, but from the inside of the tomb, there is something special happening to you!

There isn't enough preaching and teaching about Saturday seasons. You should know that there are seasons in your life that feel like Holy Saturday, with no hope for coming back, no sign of life, no evidence of a prophecy coming to pass, and no external signal that things are about to turn around.

You need to know that advantageous adversity also gives you the privilege of insider information. The seal and the stone on your recovery cave will not allow people to see what God is doing in your life behind closed doors. You would be wise not to disclose these things.

Most people do not know how to handle someone who is recovering; they only know how to handle someone who has recovered. Be honest—you would be much more comfortable around a recovered alcoholic than a recovering alcoholic. You would be more comfortable around a recovered drug addict than a recovering drug addict. In fact, many people would not feel comfortable telling someone else what they are actively recovering from. We like victors, conquerors, and champions. We want to know what you have beaten or conquered, not what you are actively fighting.

While you are recovering, remain silent until God raises you on Sunday. Get the most out of your Saturday season! Saturday seasons are one of the most important seasons of your life!

One of Peter's sermonic texts on the day of Pentecost gives us some insight into the mystery of Saturday seasons. He told the crowd on the day of Pentecost that God would not "suffer thine Holy One to see corruption" (Acts 2:27).

The Jews believed that, once a body was dead, it would take three days before the body began to erode and decompose. They called the decomposition process a process of corruption. That was why Mary and Martha did not want to remove the stone from Lazarus's tomb. He had been dead for four days, which means he would have begun to decompose and stink as a result.

God's "Holy One," however, would die but not suffer corruptions of his flesh and bones, because the Father would not allow it. Peter's choice of text from the book of Psalms implicitly prophesies that God's "Holy One" would not spend more than three days in the grave.

God allowed his son to suffer pain, but not corruption. He was bruised and wounded, but not corrupted.

Holy hardship will not allow you to be corrupted. You may suffer pain. You may endure injury and wounding, but once you have given up the ghost and allowed the caretakers to help you move on, God will ensure that you are not corrupted by what you have experienced. God will not allow your trauma to triumph over you.

God has planned that your recovery includes a Saturday season. Saturday was the Sabbath for the Jews. It was a day of rest! God sanctified a day of rest for humanity so that we might be refreshed and restored for the next week's work. Sabbath was not about what you were resting from but what you were resting for! Your Saturday is preparing you for Sunday!

The Sabbath was not a day to be lazy but a day to be refreshed, replenished, and restored for the next week's work. The Sabbath was a day of recovery.

Your Saturday season may look like nothing to others outside of the tomb, but on the inside, God is actively restoring you so that you do not succumb to the corruption of bitterness, despair, and revenge.

You need to surrender to your Saturday season. Do not rush it; enjoy it. Holy Saturday is a full day. It is absent of the work of salvation and the work of resurrection. Once you have surrendered and given up the ghost, it is your job to recover. Your job is to rest and be refreshed. Enjoy your Saturday season for however long it lasts.

When the Father resurrects you, make sure you have taken advantage of a full season of recovery. Your Saturday season was given to you to free you of bitterness, resentment, malice, vindictiveness, and despair. Be patient, play dead, and stay surrendered. You will need to be fully rested to enjoy the reward of your suffering.

HEARING YOUR
FATHER'S VOICE

New life does not begin with sight; it begins with sound. New life does not start in the light; it starts in the dark. The late hours of Holy Saturday night prepare you to hear the voice of God take the doom out of the darkness and create in you a brand-new life.

In Chapter Five, I shared with you a few things about the hour of darkness. Jesus shared a few words about the hour of darkness to ease the angst of his disciples who were witnessing his arrest. Why would such an admonishment or disclosure be encouraging?

In the moment, I am sure that Jesus's words did not seem to offer any comfort. The dark conspiracy of the chief priest and elders of Israel was out in the open and public.

Unfortunately, the open exposure of their agenda was not met with any opposition or surprise. Darkness was being exposed for what it was, but no one was trying to halt the darkness's agenda.

There was another time in Scripture when darkness was allowed to have free rein. Genesis 1:2 tells us that, in the beginning, "the earth was without form, and void," and that "darkness was upon the face of the deep." In the beginning, before God spoke the words, "Let there be light" (Gen. 1:3), darkness was out in the open and was the primary cause of the void and emptiness of the earth.

The darkness in the beginning, as well as the hour of darkness during the time of Jesus's passion, was not just the absence of natural light, but also the absence of theological light. Darkness is the absence of truth. Darkness is the absence of distinction and discernment. Darkness is not the presence of anything, but the absence of something.

Darkness is created by an absence of light: the light of God and his Word. In the beginning, darkness was having its say on the earth. The context for God's creative work in Genesis was darkness. In other words, the new world was formed after dark.

God did not begin the work of creation in the light. He began his creative work in the dark. He started in the primordial darkness that was filled with nothingness.

God beginning in the dark explains the significance of the day beginning in the evening instead of the morning, according to Genesis 1. God does not begin new things in the light; he starts new things in the dark. Jesus's words about the hour of darkness were not just a declaration of doom, but also a proclamation of hope. The devil was doing an old thing, but God was about to do a new thing.

The hour of darkness was dark, decadent, and diabolical. It was also the perfect time for God to do a new thing. We often have it twisted and backward when we think that darkness means the end of a thing. The Bible seems to suggest that darkness is actually the beginning of a new thing.

The cross and resurrection of Jesus Christ takes the doom out of darkness and gives us hope of a new beginning. Your darkest moments in life were not a dismal ending but a delightful beginning. Just as the days of creation start with the evening and end in the morning, so does your discipleship as a son and daughter of God. Your journey does not end in the dark; it starts there. Peter declares that we have been brought out of the darkness into the marvelous light (1 Pet. 2:9). Sovereign suffering starts with darkness but ends in glorious light.

Matthew, Mark, and Luke all disclose a detail about Jesus's crucifixion. In each of their passion narratives, they tell us there was darkness over the earth from the sixth to the ninth hour.

Could it be that the darkness from the sixth to the ninth hour is akin to the primordial darkness of Genesis 1? The death of Jesus Christ happened under the cover of a dark sky, signifying the beginning of a new thing! As the scriptures declare, the veil in the temple was rent during the three-hour darkness (Mark 15:33–38). The veil of the old covenant was rent, and the new covenant was about to begin.

God turns darkness into day. He does not need light to bring about new life. He has the power to start a new thing in the dark.

The darkness of Genesis 1, the darkness from the sixth hour to the ninth hour, and the darkness of your pain are all eradicated by the same thing: the voice of God. Darkness never has the last say. Darkness turns into day when the God who was silent at night begins to speak, ushering in the joy that comes in the morning!

Sovereign Silence

If God began creation with a word to "Let there be light," then a characteristic of the primordial darkness was the absence of sovereign sound! Your hour of darkness is no different. Sovereign suffering involves a sovereign silence. At a time when you feel like you need God's voice the most, you will listen for him and hear nothing.

Before the restorative voice of the Father sounds off to inaugurate the new creation, you must endure a season of sovereign silence. Your holy hardship involves loud enemies and silent partners.

What makes this kind of sovereign silence so deafening and debilitating is the contrast with how God spoke to and about you in previous seasons of life. It is one thing to experience sovereign silence if you have never heard his voice. It is a totally different issue when you were accustomed to hearing from God frequently.

At the resurrection of Lazarus, Jesus was grateful that his Father heard him. Jesus had such an enviable prayer life that the disciples sought Jesus to teach them how to pray. Jesus's birth was announced, and his ministry was replete with revelation and affirmation from the Father. Unfortunately, at an appointed time, the voice that affirmed him at the river and on a mountain was silent when Jesus could have used it the most.

Your darkest season will also involve a unique silence, when God is silent. The volume of revelation and spiritual information dries up during your trouble. During my holy hardship, I would pray and ask God about my trouble, and he would not answer me at all. I would ask him, What is next for me? How is this going to work out? And he remained silent. This continued for more than three months. I had heard about God being silent before, but I had never experienced it.

The emotions that rise to the surface during a dark season of sovereign silence cannot be simulated. The feelings of abandonment and forsakenness are real, and only sovereign silence can bring those emotions to bear. You do not have the power to say "you must trust him when you cannot trace him" until you have experienced sovereign silence and trusted God anyway.

Sovereign silence does not come to test your hearing; it happens to test your trust. Is God present when you can't feel him? Is God good when he doesn't respond to your cry? Is God still great when it seems as if he has left you in your enemies' hands and is providing no way of escape? Can you trust God when he is keeping you in the dark?

Jesus and his cross show us another aspect of his relationship with the Father. He reveals to us that sons and daughters of God must learn how to handle God's Word and God's silence. Jesus shows us this perfectly, but we have seen it before.

The Time of Testing
Isaac, the son of Abraham, was on his way to worship on a mountain with his father. He thought he and Abraham were

going to worship God together. He had no clue that he was the offering. Abraham told Isaac enough to keep him on the journey, but he did not tell him everything. Abraham kept Isaac in the dark.

Abraham did this intentionally. When Isaac noticed that the lamb for the sacrifice was missing, he took inventory of the things he and his father were taking up the mountain. He asked his father, Where is the lamb for the burnt offering? Abraham replied with an encrypted answer: "God will provide himself a lamb" (Gen. 22:8).

Abraham may not have known at the time that he was speaking prophetically. Even if he had known, he would have been seeing "through a glass, darkly" (1 Cor. 13:12). God did provide a ram, but neither Isaac nor Abraham knew that the ram would be in the bush.

Isaac had to trust his father when the time came to lay on the altar of sacrifice. Abraham put Isaac on the altar because he heard from God. Isaac got on the altar because he heard from his father. The narrative is not just about Abraham being tested as a father; it's about Isaac being tested as a son. In this way, Isaac was a type of Jesus Christ. He was being "obedient unto death" (Phil. 2:8). Isaac had to trust the last word he heard from his father, that God himself would provide the offering.

During that episode, as Isaac was being prepared to be sacrificed, there are no words recorded from God or Abraham. They were silent. The text provides for us no detail of the dialogue between Isaac and Abraham as Isaac was laid bound on the altar. It is safe to assume that Abraham followed through on what God told him to do without saying a word to Isaac. No explanation. No encouragement. Isaac was either anesthetized by some rock to his head, or he was wide awake to see his father raise his hand holding the blade to sacrifice him.

Given the language of Genesis 22, it would seem that Isaac stayed on the altar until his father took him off of the altar. Isaac stayed on the altar until God spoke to his father again. Genesis 22:10–13 shares with us that God did not speak again until after Abraham had taken the knife to slay his son. God did not speak until the last minute, but he did eventually speak.

What is interesting about the narrative is that it is not clear whether Isaac could hear what the Lord told Abraham. Isaac may have never heard from God directly at all during the entire episode. However, Isaac would have heard directly from his father. Eventually, the same father that put him on the altar would have told him to get off the altar. God and Abraham would not always be silent.

God's silence is not testing your hearing; it is testing your trust. Amid conflicting emotions and the darkness of despair and depression, will you continue to trust the Father? Can you trust a God you can't always trace? Jesus did. Isaac did. You have the power, too. Your Father may be silent now, but he will not remain silent! There will be a time when God speaks to you. It may be at the last minute, but one minute is all God needs to turn adversity into an advantage.

He Will Not Remain Silent

God's silence is reasonable and seasonal! You must believe that God's silence is only temporary. We do not have any information or instruments to calculate how long the earth was without form and void. We have no way to determine the length of time darkness covered the deep. We do, however, know that regardless of how long the darkness covered the earth, eventually God broke his silence and the darkness. God's Word has power. What he speaks has power, as well as what he has spoken.

When the devil tempted the Lord by asking him to turn the stones into bread, Jesus responded, "Man shall not live by bread alone, but by every word that proceedeth out of the mouth of God" (Matt. 4:4). Jesus overcame what the devil was saying in the present with what God said in the past. God's prior declaration still has power in the present. When you cannot hear what God is saying now, rely on what God has spoken to you before.

In fact, you can be assured that God will speak to you again, because God has spoken to you before. In other words, the last thing God said to you will not be the last thing God says to you. Hold on to the last thing God said to you before things went dark. There is revelation in your reflection and remembrance.

Jesus promised that the Holy Spirit would "bring all things to your remembrance" (John 14:26), which includes all the things Jesus has told and taught us. The work of the Holy Ghost is not restricted to present and future revelation; he can also bring things to your mind that God has said to you in the past. In a season of sovereign silence, rest in your remembrance. You will find that what God said to you promises that he will speak to you in the future!

God promised his son that he would raise him from the dead. The promise of the Father is not annulled by darkness. God's Word is still good, especially when things are bad. You must retain what God has told you in the past when he is not telling you anything now.

God's promise to you requires that he speak again. He promised that if you suffer with him, you will reign with him. His Word declares that the fellowship of his suffering is joined to the power of his resurrection. The silence of the season is a precursor for the resounding voice of God to speak to you, transforming ruin into reign!

Prophecy and the promise of fulfillment provide the hope that the silent God of our suffering will not remain silent. God's silence is only a selah, a musical rest or pause before the next word he speaks. In music, the rest adds tension into the story the composer is telling through their music. God's silence adds tension to your story. You cannot have tension without two end points. In other words, as the rest in music comes in between two notes, so also does God's silence come in between instances of speaking.

God is going to speak again! The fulfillment of his promise will come. As Habakkuk tells us, a vision of God has power no matter how long it takes to be fulfilled: "For the vision is yet for an appointed time, but at the end it shall speak, and not lie: though it tarry, wait for it; because it will surely come, it will not tarry" (Hab. 2:3). The lies of the darkness will not have the last say. Darkness obscures reality. Darkness hides, deceives, and conceals. Your life will not end that way. God will speak again. His voice will create life and light. His truth will ultimately be proclaimed. His truth will ultimately prevail. He will not remain silent.

What to Expect when He Speaks

When God speaks after a season of sovereign silence, you can expect illumination and revelation. After he speaks, you will not be in the dark anymore. You will not be ignorant of the power of God or his love for you. The voice of the Lord is going to expose, illuminate, and reveal.

Light is necessary for sight. When the Father speaks, expect eye-opening experiences. Your eyes will open long before your metaphorical tomb opens.

The Genesis account of the creation exposes a caveat about our physical world. Light was created on the first day, but the sun and moon were created on the fourth day. Physics suggests that the speed of light in the natural world is 186,282 miles per second. The light from which that speed was calculated is the light of our sun.

According to Genesis, there is another light that preceded the light of our sun. The first light of creation would have moved at least at the same speed of the light of our sun. However, that light succeeded the sound of his voice. In nature, light moves faster than sound, but when it comes to his voice, sound moves faster than light.

This suggests that you may hear from God long before you see the evidence of what he has said. Because natural light follows divine sound, your situation must catch up to your revelation. Your circumstance must catch up to God's sound. Like Elijah in 1 Kings 18, you will hear an abundance of rain long before you see a cloud the size of a man's hand. Do not be discouraged because you do not yet see the light. Rejoice because you have heard the sound. It is only a matter of time before your circumstance manifests what your spirit has heard.

The Father's voice, according to Hebrews, is "quick"; it is faster than the speed of light and is also adept at "dividing asunder" (Heb. 4:12). After God said, "Let there be light," he separated light from darkness. When God speaks, you should expect to experience some separation from darkness.

One of the theological characteristics of darkness is that it obscures truth. Darkness conceals. It is a safe place for falsehoods to rule. The darkness lies. Light, however, brings about distinction and revelation, thereby exposing the lies that lived in darkness. God's voice separates truth from lie. More powerfully, the point of light is not to expose the lie, but to reveal truth.

The passion of Jesus Christ, like your sovereign suffering, is a trial of identity. The questions the devil, the chief priest, and Pilate asked Jesus all involved a question of Jesus's identity. They all wanted to know if he was the Son of God (Matt 4:6; Matt. 26:63; John 19:7–9). His conviction and execution were human judgment on that claim. The chief priest who brought him to Pilate believed that Jesus's claim to sonship was a falsehood. However, the light of the first day of the week exposed that Jesus was not a charlatan parading around Jerusalem as a false messiah. The dawn of the first day of the week exposed the falsity of the chief priest's charges and the truth of Jesus's claim.

Your trials have not been about sin, but sonship. Your suffering is really a test to see if you are who God says you are. Regardless of the accusations you have endured and the self-doubt you have succumbed to, the voice of the Lord will soon reveal that you are indeed a son or daughter of God. God's voice affirms truth and negates lies.

You can hear the affirming voice of God when Genesis says, "And God saw the light, that it was good" (Gen. 1:4). You can expect the Father's voice to affirm the truth that it reveals. You can expect to hear God say, "You're good." You have endured something terrible. You have been the victim of heinous accusations and trials. Through all the bad, you will ultimately come out good.

When God speaks, you should not expect to hear the voice of ridicule or condemnation. Expect to hear the Father voicing his affirmation. Expect to hear what Jesus heard at the beginning of his ministry: "This is my beloved Son, in whom I am well pleased" (Matt. 3:17). The resurrection affirms and confirms what God said about Jesus in the beginning of the gospel narratives. In other words, the passion did not change the truth of how the Father felt about the Son.

Near the end of that parable of the lost son, we see the father and the prodigal son reunited in an embrace. A celebration ensued, and the father initiated it with his voice, saying, "And bring hither the fatted calf, and kill it; and let us eat, and be merry: For this my son was dead, and is alive again" (Luke 15:23–24). The lost son's father likened his return home to a resurrection. The lost son found out upon his return that his father had not changed how he felt about him. If being prodigal does not change how an earthly father feels about his son, then surely holy hardship will not change how your heavenly Father feels about you.

The voice of God activates the light and affirms its goodness, but there is more to expect when you hear God's voice piercing through the darkness. The "Let there be" in the creation narrative shows us the activating power of God's voice. The "saw . . . that it was good" (1:4) of Genesis shows us the affirming power of God's vision. But God has more to say than "Let there be" and more to see than "it was good." He also says, "bring forth" (Gen. 1:24).

Whereas God's "let there be" activates and his "that's good" affirms, the "bring forth" he utters on the third day awakens. When God speaks, expect activation. When God sees, expect affirmation. When God speaks again, expect an awakening!

Your Time to Bring Forth

Jesus shared with his disciples, "The hour is come, that the Son of man should be glorified. Verily, verily, I say unto you, Except a corn of wheat fall into the ground and die, it abideth alone: but if it die, it bringeth forth much fruit" (John 12:23–24). Jesus likened his death to a grain of wheat falling into the ground and being dead and buried. He likened the resurrection to the seed bringing forth a harvest.

The resurrection of Jesus of Nazareth was the bringing forth of the first fruit of the dead. As a matter of fact, the scriptures tell us that there were many people seeing resurrected people walking in Jerusalem after Jesus's resurrection (Matt. 27:53). Jesus died alone but was raised with a harvest of first fruits unto the Father.

Viewing the resurrection as the harvesting of seed opens a window to see the creation narrative in Genesis as a type of resurrection. The Bible says, in Genesis 1:11–13:

> And God said, Let the earth bring forth grass, the herb yielding seed, and the fruit tree yielding fruit after his kind, whose seed is in itself, upon the earth: and it was so. And the earth brought forth grass, and herb yielding seed after his kind, and the tree yielding fruit, whose seed was in itself, after his kind: and God saw that it was good. And the evening and the morning were the third day.

On the third day, God spoke to the ground of the earth so that it would yield the first harvest. The fruit that was brought forth that day was the first fruits of the earth. The ground was nurturing seed that God had planted. On the third day of creation, God, with his words, awakened the grass, herb, and trees of the earth.

I believe that the third day of creation was a type of resurrection of Christ. Jesus was the first fruit of a harvest, and he was raised on the third day. Jesus likened his death to the death of a corn of wheat and the resurrection to a harvest. Jesus's resurrection represented the dawn of a new creation.

The voice that awakened the corn of wheat nestled in the ground on the third day of creation is the same voice that awakened the first fruit of the resurrection. The voice that awakened the wheat was the same voice that sourced the wheat. The voice that awakened the seed in Genesis is the voice that planted it.

During your holy hardship, you surrendered to God and died to self. You gave up the ghost to be metaphorically buried and play dead. You may have also felt like you were buried in despair, hopelessness, and powerlessness. However, when the voice of God says "bring forth," your eyes will open to the truth. You were not buried. You were planted. Your holy hardship leads to a harvest of holiness.

As your situation during holy hardship looked to you and others, so also the ground presented no signs of life in the creation narrative. The ground and the seed in it were figuratively dead. God's voice raised the dead seeds in the ground to life. You learn during advantageous adversity that the seeds of love, joy, peace, long-suffering, gentleness, goodness, faith, meekness, and temperance that were planted in you spring up into new life. The trouble fertilizes the fruit of the Spirit that is planted in you.

As you remain in the cave of surrender, as you continue to play dead, you will find that some voices just do not awaken you. There may be the voices of people you love. There may be the voices of people who love you, but no matter how much encouragement they give you, their voices do not awaken you to new life!

An awakening voice can cause you to bring forth new life after death. You must realize that Jesus was not raised to the life he had before his death. Jesus was raised to new life. God does not want to restore you back to normal. His voice has the power to renew you and give you a life that is much better than normal.

Awakening voices are heard through the people in your life who have spiritual authority over you. The voice that can raise you from the dead is the voice of a person to whom you have spiritually submitted. Jesus, as the Son of God, was fully submitted to the Father.

Awakening voices can cause you to "bring forth" because voices with spiritual authority carry a measure of the Spirit's authority. According to Jesus, that authority is to give life (John 6:63). New life on the earth starts in the Spirit.

The Spirit gave life to the first Adam. The Spirit gave life to the awaiting army in the valley of dry bones. The Spirit gave life to the body of Jesus Christ in the tomb. The Spirit will also give you new life after a season of hardship.

The Spirit of God is represented by breath and wind in Scripture. Breath is the wind needed to speak. Awakening voices are those voices that have the Spirit of God on their breath. Please do not limit them to a certain gender, age, or social class. The power of the voice does not come from demographic classifications of the vessel. In the same way the powerful sound of a trumpet is not sourced by the trumpet but by the wind that blows through it, the power in the vessel of the awakening voices is in the wind or the Spirit that flows through them.

I did not mention this earlier, but I should mention it now—before God spoke in Genesis 1, the Spirit moved. Be encouraged, because if you can feel the Spirit, the wind of God, get ready to hear the Word of God. My suffering season shifted into a bring-forth season when I began to sense the wind of God and hear the Word of God through the voices of my spiritual leaders. My biological father, my pastor, and my bishop were instrumental in restoring me back to normal and eventually to better than normal. They have all endured their own sovereign suffering and come out of those seasons better than normal. They knew what it felt like and could guide me through the process, while recognizing when the process had finished its course.

Sometimes I was awakened to bring forth through one-on-one conversation with my father or pastor. Other times, I was awakened through the sermons and teachings of my bishop. Their objective was not only to teach me things, but to impart life into me and help raise me from pain into power. They were the voices that affirmed me in life and ministry. They were used by God to awaken me to new life after adversity.

Awakening voices are powerful because they are communicated and heard through relationship, not just rhetoric. Your resurrection will be facilitated by relationship and revelation. You do not come back from holy hardship just because of what you have learned. You are raised from the dead because of how you are loved!

Awakening voices will persuade you "that neither death, nor life, nor angels, nor principalities, nor powers, nor things present, nor things to come, nor height, nor depth, nor any other creature, shall be able to separate us from the love of God, which is in Christ Jesus our Lord" (Rom. 8:38–39). As the hymn writer said of being saved, I now sing about being delivered from holy hardship: "Love lifted me. Love lifted me. When nothing else could help, Love lifted me."[1] The love of God communicated through the awakening voices of spiritual leaders will lift you from your adversity, too.

NOTE

[1] James Rowe, "Love Lifted Me," 1912.

YOUR NEXT STEPS
AFTER RESURRECTION

The risen Jesus is full of surprises. I am not stating hyperbole or a subjective opinion about the risen Jesus's surprising attributes. The Bible gives accounts of how Jesus surprised those he chose to appear to after being raised from the dead. Given the public shame Jesus endured, it might surprise you that Jesus did not roll up to Herod or Pilate's palace to parade his new life and powers in front of them. Neither did Jesus disrupt the liturgical responsibilities of the chief priest after getting up with all power in heaven and in earth. Jesus did not even pay one visit to the Roman soldiers who mocked and maimed him during his passion. Jesus did not need public vindication for his public humiliation.

Another surprise about the risen Jesus is the fact that he was not seeking to be worshiped either. He did not host a crusade or a conference. He had a more astonishing agenda. Instead of developing worshipers, Jesus was looking to make witnesses. Most of these eyewitness encounters were held in private, not public.

Once you are awakened to new life, you too will be mature enough to handle being privately vindicated after being publicly humiliated. You also need to be wise about who and how you allow others to witness the power of your new life. These post-resurrection encounters can teach you a lot about how to live new life after trouble and holy hardship is over.

Reintroduce Yourself

John 20:5 offers a minor detail about the state of the tomb upon its discovery by "the other disciple" (assumedly John himself). John shares with us what he saw when he stooped to look into the empty tomb: "And he stooping down, and looking in, saw the linen clothes lying." The synoptic writers do not give us this seemingly minor detail—only John does.

Myriad questions come to mind about why John would include this nugget in his resurrection narrative. In a way, this detail confirms that the body of Jesus was not stolen. Why would thieves take the time to unwrap the body of Jesus before moving it to another location?

It is apparent from John's narrative that the linen clothing was important, given the attention he gave to the process that Nicodemus and Joseph of Arimathea went through to prepare the body of Jesus of Nazareth for burial. Jesus being our high priest, as John portrayed him in his Gospel, helps explain why the clothes were left behind. According to Leviticus 16, the high priest would begin the day of atonement in his holy linen garments. He would wear a linen coat, linen breeches, and a linen mitre on his head throughout the atonement ritual (Lev. 16:4, 23).

After the work of atonement was complete, the high priest was to take off the linen garments that would have been covered with blood from the sacrifice and leave them in the tabernacle of the congregation. The bloodstained linen garments left in the sepulcher were evidence that the atonement act was complete and that that portion of our high priest's work was finished.

The natural question to ask about the next portion of the atonement liturgy is: What did Aaron change into after getting rid of the linen garments? Leviticus 16:24 says that the high priest was to "wash his flesh with water in the holy place, and put on his garments, and come forth." The high priest's clothes, according to Exodus 28:2, were made "for glory and for beauty." In the same way, Jesus left the bloodstained linen garments behind as evidence that his work was finished and that he had been glorified and beautified.

He went into the grave one way and exited the grave transformed and glorified. The change in garments was an indication of a transformation. The transformation was so stark that Mary Magdalene did not recognize Jesus when she saw him at the sepulcher. The Bible says she looked at him, "supposing him to be the gardener" (John 20:15). Jesus's glorification and beautification were so overwhelming that people close to him could not recognize him.

After your season of suffering, you will enjoy the overwhelming process of glorification and beautification. However, like Jesus, people will not recognize you at first, and you will have to reintroduce yourself.

Your reintroduction into your community of family and friends will require that you understand, as Jesus did, that his work on the cross was finished, but his work as the risen Son was not. Jesus still had work to do. He had to ascend and ultimately sit at the right hand of God the Father. His work was not done; as a matter of fact, in a certain respect, it was only beginning.

A season of sovereign suffering once consummated by a season of glorification and beautification commenced another season of work in a glorified state. Jesus could not ascend without being resurrected. Jesus could not sit at the right hand of God in his pre-resurrected form. The resurrection was a necessity for the next work Jesus had to do.

Your holy hardship and the power that you are now privileged to have are prerequisites for the work you have been destined to do. Your work is not over; it has only just begun. The devastation of your suffering prepared you for the glorification of your destiny.

The power of the resurrection has come upon you to shift you into your new work. Your glorification and beautification clothed you with the glory and honor necessary to be fruitful and productive. You survived so you could thrive. Now you must do the hard work of reintroducing yourself to people who were once very familiar with you.

Do not expect everyone to embrace the new you initially. The truth is, the people you are reintroducing yourself to did not expect you to bounce back. They thought you were finished. Mary Magdalene was expecting to take care of a dead Jesus, not encounter a living and glorified Jesus. Expect people to be surprised, shocked, and a little taken aback. They may mistake you for someone else, just as Mary mistook Jesus for being the gardener. You should expect to be treated differently because you are different.

Now that you have received the power of the resurrection to a new way of life and work, you should expect people to treat you like they are not familiar with you. It is a responsible thing for people who were familiar with the old you to behave like they are not familiar with the new you.

Here is why: a change in garment represents a change in responsibility. Your new way of being and the power you have received comes with a new responsibility and a new work.

The Bible uses the change in garment to symbolize a shift in responsibility and mindset. Joseph, upon being promoted in Egypt, received new garments. Aaron, upon being consecrated to high priest, had to take off the slave garments of Egypt and place on himself the holy garments of glory and beauty. The prodigal son, upon his return, was stripped of his old clothes and given a robe and a ring. Blind Bartimaeus, upon being called to Jesus, took off his beggar's garment. Jesus shifted from master to servant when he washed the disciples' feet by girding himself with a towel. Whenever the garments change, responsibility shifts, and it requires that the person undergoing the shift understand that they are no longer familiar to the people they were once very familiar with.

Familiarity will undermine the power of your resurrection. My advice to you is that during your reintroduction, be cordial, not common.

Your new work, new responsibility, and new authority requires that you operate in old relationships with new honor and new boundaries. You have been changed. Your conversations must change. Your attitude must change. Your actions must change. Nothing says *I am the same old person I was before I went through the pain* than a lack of change in one's behavior.

You are better than normal, which means you are not normal. Be cordial, but do not diminish the authority you now walk in with actions that make you look like the same old person you were before you went through your holy hardship.

I Am Not Ready Yet

In John's resurrection narrative, the revelation of Jesus's identity to Mary caused her to reach out to touch Jesus. What is intriguing about Mary's reaction is not the swift shift from grief to joy upon learning that the Lord was alive and conversing with her, but Jesus's response to Mary's attempted embrace.

After long periods of separation from loved ones or a long trial that put you in a place where the people you love could not touch or hug you, it is customary or common to embrace the rejuvenated, healed, and restored loved one. It would be normal for someone you have not seen since your season of suffering to want to hug you when they realize that you have come back from surgery, deployment, unemployment, or even a prison sentence. It would be customary and normal. Jesus, however, was resurrected from the dead, which is, in fact, abnormal, uncommon, and unprecedented. No wonder his response to Mary seemed uncommon and unprecedented.

Jesus told Mary, "Touch me not; for I am not yet ascended to my Father" (John 20:17). Jesus reintroduced himself to Mary but did so cordially, not according to common standards of reunion. He does not say "touch me not" and leave it at that. He offered to her the reason why she could not touch him. Here's a paraphrase of what Jesus said to her: "Don't touch me because I have yet to spend time in the presence of my Father."

In our vernacular, the word *touch* means to come in contact with physically. As you reintroduce your family and friends to the new and improved you, not only must you be careful who you come in contact with, but when you come in contact with them. You must manage your interactions with people when you have not had the time to interact with God alone.

My advice, before you come in contact with them, is to make sure you have been in contact with God. Jesus managed his former way of relating with Mary because he had not yet been in the presence of his Father. In a sense, Jesus was telling Mary, "You can't handle me right now." You must exercise wise judgment in discerning who, how, and when people can handle the glory you walk in after a season of suffering.

There are some things you will have learned that they cannot handle. There are some revelations about yourself and God that they will not be able to handle. There are some insights about old friendships and enemies you will have that your old friends just cannot handle. I encourage you to be prayerful about whom you contact and when you contact them once you have come back from metaphorical death.

There are some people you love and who love you whom you must pray for and about before you spend time interacting with them. Again, before you come in contact with them, make sure you have been in contact with God! Before you insert yourself into the world of friendships and work, make sure you pray and spend time with God.

Just as they must adjust to who you have become, you have to adjust to who you have become. Only God can help you get used to living in a new state of power, authority, and responsibility because of your holy hardship. You must embrace the truth that you are different, and you must adjust to being treated by and treating the people you love differently.

Psalm 105:15 says, "Touch not mine anointed, and do my prophets no harm." What we usually imply about this "touch" is that it comes from an ill-intentioned foe. However, given the response of Jesus to Mary Magdalene, there is a possibility that the psalmist may have had more than just foes in mind when he wrote that text.

The Greek word for *touch* used by John in John 20 is the word *haptou*, which means to fasten or to lay hold of. Mary, by implication of the word, was trying to hold Jesus. She tried to fasten herself to him. I don't blame her.

She had been looking for him, and his whereabouts were unknown. Once she found out that he was with her, it was only natural to try to embrace him in such a way as to indicate that she did not want him to leave. She wanted him to stay.

Unfortunately, that was not Jesus's purpose, nor was it his destiny. Jesus was destined to ascend and sit at the Father's right hand. Jesus was destined to leave and send back the Holy Ghost. Mary's cling revealed her desire. Jesus's response revealed his destiny.

Any touch that gets in the way of you fulfilling destiny is a touch that can do you harm. Jesus was destined to ascend, but Mary's touch was an attempt to keep him on a level she could handle. You must not allow the well-intentioned embrace of friends and family get in the way of you going to another level. It is not the touch of an enemy that you must be careful of now, but it is the clinging of well-intentioned friends that you must guard yourself against.

Your new power comes with work and responsibilities that require you to go to another level. Once your close allies find out that you are no longer suffering and in pain, they will naturally want everything to go back to normal. They may want things to go back to the way they were before. Your pain, however, gave you an advantage that beautifies and glorifies you so that things are not back to normal, but better than normal. Not all of your allies can handle your new normal.

You must make sure to be cordial to them, but not common to them. You must make sure that before you come in contact with them, you have been in contact with God. You must also beware of their attempt to keep you on a level that they can handle. You must create the necessary separation for your elevation. And there's one more thing you must do. You must create boundaries for your Mary Magdalenes, but you must also seek reconciliation with your Peters.

Forgive, But Do Not Forget

The power of the resurrection includes the power of forgiveness. Some of the people you will reintroduce yourself to are people who have trespassed against you.

It is ironic that the person who prompted the telling of the parable of the unforgiving servant was the same person who needed post-resurrection forgiveness. The parable of the unforgiving servant followed an inquiry from Peter as to how many times he should forgive his brother. Peter limited the number to seven. Jesus extended it to seventy times seven and then told the parable.

I can imagine that the parable of the unforgiving servant played in Peter's mind over and over after he denied Jesus. After more than two days of guilt, remorse, and regret, Peter got the news that Jesus's tomb was empty and that Jesus was alive. Peter did not settle for taking someone else's word for it; he ran to the tomb, according to the Gospel of John, to see for himself. Jesus was no longer there.

Peter knew what he had done a couple of days ago. He had messed up many times before, but never like this. He had been rebuked as Satan for trying to keep Jesus away from the cross. He was gently rebuked for cutting off a servant's ear. There was nothing, however, like the act of denying Jesus, especially after he boldly stated that he would do the opposite and go with Jesus to prison and death.

How would Jesus deal with Peter now that he was alive? The tension is palpable in the Gospel of John as Jesus appeared to the disciples several times after the resurrection and did not say anything to Peter directly about his denial. Jesus held Thomas accountable for the words he uttered after the resurrection. I cannot state this for sure, but I can imagine that Peter may have wondered when it would be his turn.

More than a week after Jesus's resurrection, he addressed Peter in his own way about the denial. In John 21, Jesus asked Peter if he loved him the same number of times Peter denied him. Not only did Jesus ask Peter about his love, but he also gave Peter new responsibilities and a new identity.

According to the text, after Jesus's first few appearances, Peter went back to fishing. Jesus initially called Peter from a fisherman's boat. He told Peter and some of his friends,

"Follow me, and I will make you fishers of men" (Matt. 4:19). Jesus uttered those words before his death. After his resurrection, he changed Peter's career ambitions again. No longer would Peter be a fisher of men; he would be a feeder of sheep.

Jesus understood that as he suffered to sit on the throne, Peter was being vetted for more authority as well. Jesus did not let Mary's desire for him to stay get in the way of his destiny. He also did not let Peter's denial get in the way of Peter's destiny.

Jesus forgave Peter, and you should forgive those who have trespassed against you. Maybe their trial and denial were a part of their own holy hardship, just as your suffering was a part of yours. Your Peters are not like your Judases.

Forgive your Peters. You can forgive them because the person they hurt died on Good Friday. The people who hurt the old you need to be forgiven by the new you.

The people you forgive will love you much because they have been forgiven much. I believe this is why Jesus asked Peter three times about love. Jesus knew, according to what he said in Luke's Gospel about forgiveness and love (Luke 7:47), that those who are forgiven much love much. Jesus asked Peter three times so Peter and the others could hear how much he loved Jesus. Peter could love much because he was forgiven much.

Advantageous adversity gives you a power to reconcile with those who caused you the pain. The resurrection is all about reconciliation.

My closing words to you are to forgive, but don't forget. I don't mean that in the traditional sense of forgive them, but always keep it in the back of your mind just in case they do it again. What I mean when I say forgive but don't forget is forgive the misery, but don't forget the meaning.

Your misery during the season of holy hardship has meaning. The pain you have endured during your adversity has meaning. Every situation and episode, the darkness, the celebration, the garden prayers, adversaries all around, the times when you had to engage in cross-shaped prayers, giving up the ghost, the Saturday seasons, and the Father's voice all have meaning. Forgive the misery, but don't forget the meaning of your suffering. Do not forget the meaning of your pain.

You cannot be responsible with the advantage of adversity if you forget the meaning of the privilege of pain. You have suffered for your success. You have endured for your excellence. You have been vetted for greater responsibility. You have endured too much not to enjoy the advantage of your adversity.

You Are Ready to Ascend

Only a resurrected Jesus could ascend into the clouds. Only a crucified Jesus could be resurrected. You, too, can ascend to greater heights if you allow your tribulation to fuel your transformation. I am a much better person, pastor, and professional because of my holy hardship. During that time, which, ironically, extended from Ash Wednesday to Pentecost of 2017, I learned how to handle adversity like Jesus so that I could also learn how to ascend like him. I hope the lessons and perspectives in this book have empowered you to do the same. Do not let your trouble ground you. Allow it to grow you. Seize the advantage of adversity by becoming more like Jesus, and you, too, will eventually ascend.

BIBLIOGRAPHY

Brueggemann, Walter. *Truth Speaks to Power: The Countercultural Nature of Scripture*. Louisville: Westminster John Knox Press, 2013.

Clinton, J. Robert. *The Making of a Leader: Recognizing the Lessons and Stages of Leadership Development*. Colorado Springs: NavPress, 1988.

Crouch, Andy. *Culture Making: Recovering Our Creative Calling*. Downers Grove: InterVarsity Press, 2008.

———. *Strong and Weak: Embracing a Life of Love, Risk, and True Flourishing*. Downers Grove: InterVarsity Press, 2016.

Frangipane, Francis. *The Three Battlegrounds*. Cedar Rapids: Arrow Publications, 1989.

Gansky, Alton. *40 Days: Encountering Jesus Between the Resurrection and Ascension*. Nashville: B & H Publishing Group, 2007.

Hull, Bill. *The Disciple-Making Pastor*. Grand Rapids: Baker Books, 2007.

Longfellow, Henry Wadsworth. *The Complete Poetical Works of Henry Wadsworth Longfellow*. Redditch, UK: Read Books Ltd., 2013.

Maxwell, John. *The 21 Irrefutable Laws of Leadership: Follow Them and People Will Follow You*. Nashville: Thomas Nelson, 1998.

Mowczko, Marg. "The Creed (Hymn) of Philippians 2:6–11." *Marg Mowczko* blog. May 1, 2010. Accessed February 5, 2022. https://margmowczko.com/the-creed-of-philippians-2/.

Newton, John. "Amazing Grace." 1779.

Richards, E. Randolph, and Brandon J. O'Brien. *Misreading Scripture with Western Eyes: Removing Cultural Blinders to Better Understand the Bible*. Downers Grove: InterVarsity Press, 2012.

Rowe, James. "Love Lifted Me." 1912.

Shepherd, Thomas. "Must Jesus Bear the Cross Alone?" 1693.

Tillich, Paul. *A History of Christian Thought: From Its Judaic and Hellenistic Origins to Existentialism*. New York: Simon & Schuster, 1972.

Wesley, Charles. "Father, I Stretch My Hands to Thee." 1707.

Yeago, David S. "Introduction." In *The Apostolic Faith: A Catholic and Evangelical Introduction to Christian Theology*. Unpublished manuscript. Grand Rapids: Eerdmans, n.d.

"Pastor Dicks puts to words the adversity so many of us have experienced and yet challenges us all to get up and submit to the process. The revelation and wisdom contained in these pages will change your life as well as your perspective on adversity forever."

—**Pastor Patrick A. Harvin,** Senior Pastor, Jerusalem Baptist Church, Hopkins, SC

"The depressed spiritual leader will find this book an inspiration. The author does an excellent job of translating the hurt and pain of his traumatic experiences into a potential bright future of hope. As a former depressed pastor, I would highly recommend every spiritual leader take the time to read this book—it offers excellent counsel."

—**Pastor A. A. Dicks Sr.,** 40-year Pastor of Friendship Baptist Church, Columbia, SC

"Dicks is reflective and courageous, daring to probe the most ancient issues, uncovering contemporary insights. Suffering is one such issue, which compels the consequent *why* of suffering's existence. Few have grappled with this why more than theists and atheists. To atheists, suffering repudiates God. To theists, suffering reveals God. As a courageous, thinking theist, Dicks artfully zeroes in on the redemptive effect of believers' suffering. Such a courageous perspective produces power!"

—**Bishop Michael A. Blue,** Pastor of Door of Hope Church, Marion SC; Presiding Prelate, Christian Covenant Fellowship of Ministries

"Christian faithfulness is hard to mobilize when life is not going well. Pastor Dicks says our troubles do not have to be traumatizing if we are willing to learn from the Bible's personalities and see how they made their ways through hard times. Dicks resolutely reminds us that Christian faith is not a shield against affliction. Christian discipleship does, however, provide the way through anguish and agony."

—**Rev. Ginger Barfield,** PhD, Lutheran Theological Southern Seminary, Professor of Biblical Studies and Theology, Director of Baptist Studies, Columbia, SC

"Anthony is a faithful, consistent man of God who has felt the sting of life, yet remains solid, grounded, and unmovable in the Lord. In *Holy Hardship*, you will receive instructions and truths to become enduring soldiers even while bleeding. As you allow the biblical truths in this book to change you, Acts 14:22 (NLT)—'we must suffer many hardships to enter the Kingdom of God'—will be forever etched on your heart."

—**DeWayne L. Wright,** Kingdom Living Ministries, Lead Pastor, Perth Amboy, NJ

"Rev. A. A. Dicks Jr. has written the ultimate book for advancing through adversity. This battle-tested warrior yet tenacious thought leader has written a prescription of a healing ointment after hardships. Picking up this book will surely pick you up from a fallen state."

—**Rev. Dr. Aaron R. E. Bishop,** Pastor, Grace Christian Church, Columbia, SC

"Skillfully blending the earthly life of Jesus with his own personal experience of pain and difficulty, Dicks calls the reader into a time of purposeful pondering guaranteed to change your perspective on hardship. After reading this book, you will no longer bemoan your trials but celebrate them in appreciation for how they propel you forward."

—**Bishop Kenneth M. Yelverton,** DMin, The Temple of Refuge Church, Charlotte, NC

"Every day has a bit of darkness, but A. A. Dicks shines a light on handling adversity in this book. He takes you through many stories to show how God uses challenging circumstances to create an advantage for you. You will enjoy reading about how hard times are made into a good life."

—**Jacob Coldwell,** author of *Before You Begin*

"Dicks provides a signature text built upon the simple strength of one profoundly provocative premise: trouble changes you. Therapeutic and vindicating, this narrative carries the full weight of a cleric acquainted with the inevitable adversities bound to meet any leader seeking to significantly influence community. With candor and character, Dicks gives voice to those who seek strength in times of trouble. This work is a must-read for any leader with a passion to transform community!"

—**Bishop Eric J. Freeman,** Senior Pastor, The Meeting Place Church of Greater Columbia, SC

"Those whose journey has been blanketed with distress have little issue identifying the what, but this book helps us determine the why. The author's transparency enabled me to see not just the challenge of adversity but also the transformation and triumph that becomes my advantage."

—**Rev. J. Walter Hills, II,** Senior Pastor of New Hope Missionary Baptist Church, Portland, OR

"When the enemy comes in like a flood, the Spirit of the Lord will lift a standard against him. Parts of this book have operated as that standard. It is clear from Anthony's testimony he has both the experience and the revelation to bring encouragement to those going through similar circumstances. I hope you are blessed by this book. I know I have been."

—**Pastor Don Priest,** Senior Pastor, Living Faith Church International, Petersburg, IN